I0804901

COLUMBIA CIVIL WAR LANDMARKS

Tom Elmore

THE History PRESS

Published by The History Press
Charleston, SC 29403
www.historypress.net

Front and back covers, bottom: Panoramic views of Columbia, South Carolina, before and after the fire of February 17, 1865. From *Frank Leslie's Illustrated Newspaper*, April 8, 1865. *Image courtesy of the Walker Local History Room of the Richland County (SC) Public Library.*
Back cover: Photographs of Sherman and his generals and Lieutenant General Wade Hampton III courtesy of the Library of Congress.
Unless otherwise indicated, all photographs and illustrations in this book are by the author and/or are from his personal collection.

First published 2011
Manufactured in the United States
ISBN 978.1.60949.121.5

Library of Congress Cataloging-in-Publication Data
Elmore, Tom.
Columbia Civil War landmarks / Tom Elmore.
p. cm.
Includes bibliographical references and index.
ISBN 978-1-60949-121-5
1. Columbia (S.C.)--History--Burning, 1865. 2. Columbia (S.C.)--Tours. 3. Historic sites--South Carolina--Columbia--Guidebooks. 4. Historic buildings--South Carolina--Columbia--Guidebooks. 5. Columbia (S.C.)--Buildings, structures, etc.--Guidebooks. 6. Columbia Region (S.C.)--Tours. 7. Historic sites--South Carolina--Columbia Region--Guidebooks. 8. Historic buildings--South Carolina--Columbia Region--Guidebooks. I. Title.
E477.75.E45 2011
973.7'38--dc22
2010053701

Portions of this text originally appeared in the August and September 2003 issues of *Lake Murray Magazine* and in the Winter 2004 issue of *Blue & Gray Magazine*.

Dedicated to all the history teachers who have inspired me

&

All the preservationists who fight the never-ending battle to save our past.

Contents

Preface

For over a decade I have offered slide presentations and bus tours to thousands of individuals about Columbia's role in the Civil War. Without fail, there will always be someone with ties to Columbia who will say something like, "I've driven by that place all my life and never knew that was there!"

Contrary to the common misconception that "Sherman burned it all and what Sherman did not burn, 'progress' destroyed," there are numerous Civil War–era sites in the twenty-first-century Greater Columbia area that are in varying degrees of significance, interpretation and preservation.

This guide is divided into three main parts. The first section re-creates Sherman's route into Columbia. The second identifies six geographic areas in downtown Columbia. The third is a list of outlying significant sites.

I strongly suggest that those who are not familiar with the streets of Columbia consult a city map before visiting the sites mentioned in this book. There are many websites that offer free maps and directions. In addition, hard copies can be obtained from many local gas stations and from the Columbia Convention Center and Visitors Bureau, located at 1101 Lincoln Street in the Vista.

Unless otherwise noted, all sites are on private property and not open to the public. Please do not trespass. All information is current as of time of publication.

Acknowledgements

I am indebted to the following Columbia-area individuals, institutions and organizations for helping make this book a reality:

Debra Bloom, Walker Local History Room manager, Richland County Public Library

David Brinkman, whose research in pinpointing exactly where Sherman crossed the Broad River into Columbia was featured on the PBS program *The History Detectives* in 2009

The Cayce Historical Museum in Cayce, South Carolina, in particular Mr. Leo Redman and the late Mr. Clayton Kleckley

Mike Dawson, chief executive officer of the River Alliance

J.R. Fennell, director of the Lexington County Museum

Samantha Hood of International Paper for graciously allowing me to include a photograph of Kennsington Plantation in this book

Dean Hunt, who has meticulously tracked Sherman's movements in Lexington County

The Greater Columbia Civil War Alliance and its founder, Mr. Frank Knapp

The Historic Columbia Foundation, in particular John Sherrer, director of Cultural Resources

Jim Lawracy, president, St. Columba Division, Ancient Order of Hibernians

Palmetto Camp 22 and Lt. Gen. Wade Hampton Camp 273 of the Sons of Confederate Veterans

Mary Huntt Chapter #13, Order of the Confederate Rose

Wayne Roberts, chief archaeologist, S.C. Department of Transportation

Kenneth Robinson II, past camp commander, Charles Devens Camp #10, Sons of Union Veterans of the Civil War

The South Carolina Confederate Relic Room and Military Museum, with extra special thanks to its staff members Dr. Allen Roberson, Krissy Dunn Johnson and Joe Long

The South Carolina Department of Archives and History

The University of South Carolina's Thomas Cooper Library's Irvin Department of Rare Books & Special Collections and the book and manuscript collections of the school's South Caroliniana Library

In Charleston, Mike Coker of the Historic Old Exchange Building was a big supporter of this project and opened doors for me, while Jessica Berzon of The History Press championed this project. For these two I have a large debt of gratitude.

I would be remiss if I did not acknowledge the countless number of people who have shared with me numerous tales and legends about Columbia during the time of the "Late Unpleasantness." Even if I were to remember the name of everyone who shared the stories with me (and I dare not even pretend that I do), there would not be enough space to mention them all. So to all such individuals reading this book, you have my sincere thanks.

The acknowledgements would not be complete without thanking my mother-in-law, Mrs. Pat Wood, for reviewing the text and making numerous useful suggestions, and my parents, Roy and Connie Elmore, for encouraging my love of history and supporting my book-aholic ways.

And last, but certainly not least, I owe much to my best friend, biggest cheerleader, editor and personal Ferengi, my wife, Krys, who has never wavered in her support for my writing projects and has joyfully put up with me for over fifteen years.

A Wartime Capital City

Columbia sits on the Eastern Fall Line, near the geographic center of South Carolina. In 1860, Columbia's northern, southern and eastern boundaries were wooded areas, while the Congaree River marked the western boundary.

Columbia was founded in 1786 to appease South Carolina's upstate residents who wanted the state capital moved from Charleston on the coast (then a two-week journey from the upstate) to a more central location. Most of the site chosen for the future city was on Colonel Thomas Taylor's plantation, The Plains. Taylor, an American Revolution hero, was not too impressed by Columbia, allegedly saying, "I've swapped a damn good plantation for a damn poor town!"

The city was laid out in a two square-mile grid of four hundred city blocks. Most streets were 60 feet wide to help prevent the spread of disease and, ironically, to help prevent building fires from spreading. Assembly and Senate Streets were 150 feet wide since they were intended to be the main commercial thoroughfares, but land speculation and poor drainage resulted in Richardson (now Main) and Gervais Streets being the main avenues of commerce.

By 1860 the city had become cosmopolitan. There were two daily newspapers, the *Southern Guardian* and the *Daily South Carolinian*. The editor of the latter was Henry Timrod, who is often referred to as the unofficial "Poet Laureate of the Confederacy."

Several schools and colleges were in the city, chief among them South Carolina College (the present University of South Carolina). Near Sydney

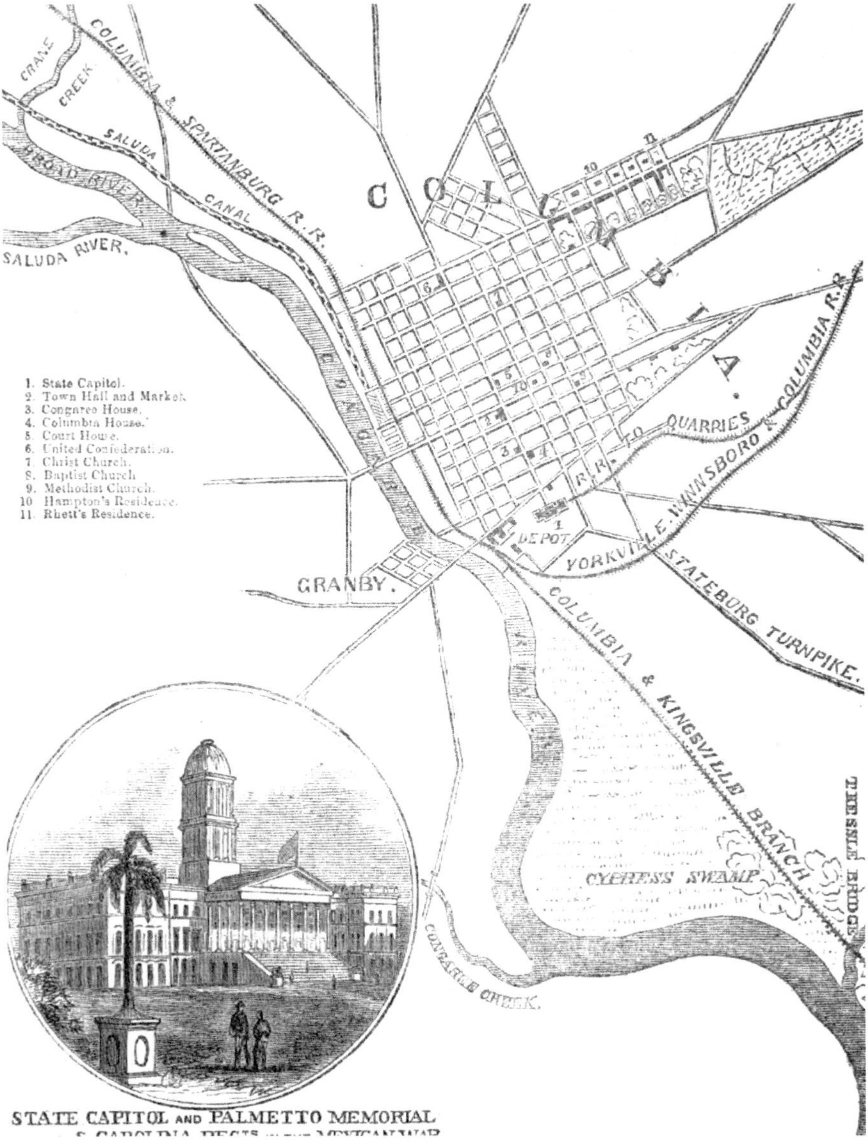

Columbia, 1865. This map, printed in *Harper's Weekly*, features an inaccurate artist's conception of the new South Carolina State House.

Park (today's Finlay Park) was the Arsenal Academy, a military prep school and the sister school to The Citadel. Both schools would play a part in the drama that unfolded. For the young women there was the Catholic-run Ursuline Convent and the Methodist Female College.

In addition, there were numerous churches of various denominations, as well as chapters and lodges of the Masons, the Odd Fellows, the Sons of Temperance and the Sons of Malta.

To an 1860 visitor to Columbia, the most striking building would have been the unfinished gray granite State House being built in the city's center next to the small, wooden structure it was replacing.

Even before the war, Columbia had a strong military presence. A prewar law required that all white males between the ages of eighteen and forty-three must serve in the militia. Consequently, there were about a half dozen militia units based in Columbia.

Patriotic support for the Confederacy was strong in Columbia. Shortly after the state seceded, a prominent Northern businessman was tarred, feathered and kicked out of town. In 1861, a barbecue was held at the state hospital to raise funds and boost support for the war effort. In 1862, amidst reports that South Carolina troops needed supplies, the Association for the Relief of Soldiers of South Carolina was formed and lasted until the war's end, raising hundreds of thousands of dollars.

Much of the patriotic flavor was due to Columbia's location. Nestled in the middle of the Confederacy's Atlantic states, Columbia was one of three untouched Confederate state capitals at the end of 1864. Although South Carolina started the Civil War, the only military action within the Palmetto State prior to 1865 had occurred in the coastal region between Charleston and Beaufort.

As one of the last Confederate manufacturing centers, Columbia was vital to the war effort. Columbia's factories produced uniforms, swords, belts, bullets, gunpowder and cannonballs. Professor Joseph LeConte of South Carolina College operated the Confederate War Department's chemical lab at the State Fairground, which produced medicines, alcohol, silver nitrate and chloroform. The Columbia Canal was leased to the Confederate government to erect powder works, which operated until 1865.

Currency, postage stamps and bonds were printed at the Confederate Treasury printing plant, where a host of "Treasury Girls" signed the increasingly worthless Confederate currency in an attempt to prevent counterfeiting.

The city's most important assets were the three railroads leading into Columbia: the Charlotte, the Greenville and the South Carolina, the latter connecting Columbia to Charleston and Augusta, Georgia. Items from Atlanta and Augusta (where the Confederate Armory was located) were shipped to General Robert E. Lee's Army of Northern Virginia through the Capital City.

Given all of this, it is not surprising that Major General William T. Sherman said of Columbia in 1865, "Richmond is not more vital to [Jefferson Davis]'s cause than Columbia and the Heart of South Carolina." Most Columbians, however, felt that Charleston, where the guns fired on Fort Sumter to start the war, was the town that the North wanted.

Columbia also held important symbolic value to the Confederacy. The First Baptist Church of Columbia was where the Secession Convention first met before adjourning to Charleston.

Columbia's inflation was out of control. In January 1862, $120 in Confederate notes equaled $100 in gold. By January 1864, $1,800 in currency was worth $100 in gold. By December it was $2,800. From then on, inflation raced even faster. It took $3,400 in currency to buy $100 in gold in January 1865, and $5,000 the next month.

This inflation was reflected in the prices of food and other goods. In 1863, corn went for $25.00 a bushel. Bacon went from $1.00 a pound in 1863 to $5.00 a pound in 1864. By 1864, eggs were $2.50 a dozen, butter $7.00 a pound and sugar $8.00 a pound. Tea, depending on the quality, was $15.00 to $25.00 a pound, and cloth was $40.00 a yard. Boots were $90.00 a pair in 1864, but they would go as high as $250.00. Flour went for $1,200.00 a barrel. In late January 1865, corn was $40.00 a bushel. In 1864 wood went for $34.00 a cord; by January 1865, it was $100.00. Candles cost $2.00 apiece. Of course, these prices were only good if you could find these items, which was often difficult.

Conversely, a common laborer earned ten dollars a day, while a skilled laborer could get fifteen dollars a day. A Confederate private earned eleven dollars a month, if and when he got paid.

Confederate General Joseph Johnston, who moved to Columbia in the fall of 1864 to be near friends and family, found living in Columbia expensive even on his salary of $300 a month. He complained in January 1865, "The expenses of living here are much above our means. We can't remain here three months longer, even with Sherman's consent."

Emma LeConte, the teenage daughter of Professor Joseph LeConte of South Carolina College, wrote in her diary in January 1865, "We live poorly. Two meals a day. Two plates of bread for breakfast…Dinner consists of a very small piece of meat, generally beef, a few potatoes and a dish of hominy and a pone of corn bread." She was better off than most people, because they had a cow and could still get butter. She noted, "Many have not tasted meat for months."

Because Charleston was under constant attacks by both the Federal navy and army, Charlestonians sent their valuables to the "safety" of Columbia for storage and protection. Among the more popular items sent away for safety were alcoholic beverages. Greed more than thirst was the reason Charlestonians saved their alcohol. In 1862, the Confederate government tried to promote food crop production by instituting a ban on the distillation of liquor from grains, fruits and potatoes. Consequently, the price of whiskey in the South jumped from twenty-five cents a gallon in 1861 to twenty-five dollars a gallon in 1865.

As Sherman got closer and closer to Savannah, the number of people seeking security in Columbia grew. Columbia's prewar population of 8,052 (of whom 3,500+ were black) had more than doubled to almost 20,000 people by the beginning of 1865. This influx of humanity meant that in 1865 there were no more houses available for rent, creating a serious housing crunch.

However, these problems would be nothing compared to those the town was about face.

Part One

Sherman Invades Columbia

In December 1864, Major General William Tecumseh Sherman (1820–1891) presented U.S. President Abraham Lincoln with a Christmas gift of Savannah, Georgia. With the completion of his "march to the sea" and the capture of the coastal town, South Carolinians knew that they were next.

Government officials in Richmond and Columbia did little to prepare the state for an invasion by Sherman's sixty-thousand-plus-man army. Just days before Sherman entered Columbia, military and government leaders issued proclamations that the city was in no danger. Many were convinced that the numerous rivers and swamps that Sherman would have to ford between Savannah and Columbia would discourage him and his army, forcing them to turn back. Strengthening this belief was the fact that South Carolina and Georgia were experiencing the wettest winter in two decades, raining twenty-eight of the first forty-five days of 1865, delaying Sherman's invasion plans by at least two weeks.

However, the South's military leaders underestimated Sherman, one of the most brilliant strategists of the war and a master motivator of men. The 1840 West Point graduate had spent much of his early military career at Fort Moultrie, outside Charleston, South Carolina. After thirteen years in the army, he sought more lucrative opportunities in the civilian world to support his wife, Ellen, and their growing family. After disappointing stints in law and banking, he became president of the newly founded Louisiana State Seminary of Learning and Military Academy (modern Louisiana State University) until Louisiana seceded from the Union.

Sherman and his generals. Seated left to right are Major Generals John Logan, William T. Sherman and Henry Slocum. Standing left to right are Major Generals Oliver O. Howard, William B. Hazen, Jefferson C. Davis and Joseph Mower. *Courtesy of the Library of Congress.*

When the war started, Sherman returned to the military. From 1862 to 1863, Sherman commanded the Fifteenth Corps and, in late 1863, headed the Army of the Tennessee. In early 1864, he became commander of the Union Military Division of the Mississippi, commanding Federal troops in an area bounded by the Mississippi River, the Gulf of Mexico, the Atlantic Ocean and most of the territory south of Virginia.

Sherman's men loved him and had full confidence in their commander. He once bragged, "I hear the soldiers talk as I ride by, 'There goes the old man. All's right.' Not a waver, doubt or hesitation when I order, and men march to certain death without a murmur when I call on them, because they know I value their lives as much as my own."

Governor Andrew Gordon Magrath was one of the few Confederate officials to realize the Palmetto State's danger. After sending numerous requests to Richmond begging for more troops to defend the state, the governor received a reply from General Robert E. Lee in late January

1865. Lee wrote that there were no troops to spare and that if he came down to South Carolina to fight Sherman, Grant would follow him and the state would be trapped between the two large Union armies.

General P.G.T. Beauregard. *From the National Archives.*

Lee did send a brigade of infantry and Major General Matthew C. Butler's cavalry division, along with Lee's cavalry chief and Columbia native Lieutenant General Wade Hampton III. Though Richmond estimated that there were 35,000 Confederate troops in the Palmetto State, 20,000 was a far more accurate number, with half in Charleston and the rest badly scattered across the state. Though attempts were made to raise local militia units, one Confederate official lamented that there were only 1,450 able-bodied men in all of South Carolina who were not currently serving in the Confederate army.

Lieutenant General Wade Hampton III. *Courtesy of the Library of Congress.*

To make a bad situation worse, Confederate General Pierre Gustave Toutant Beauregard, commander of all the Confederate forces in South Carolina, had become ill. Furthering the state's woes, his second in command, Lieutenant General William Hardee, was coming down with typhoid fever. Hardee commanded the Charleston garrison, consisting of ten thousand men, and ignored Beauregard's orders to send his men to Columbia for defense of the state's capital. Consequently, little was done to fortify or defend the city. Nevertheless, there was a strong sense on both sides that Columbia would not fall without a fight.

Hampton made what few preparations he could to defend Columbia. He suggested that Sherman's wings be attacked one by one (a move that most historians agree was the best response that the Confederates could have made). Though Hampton claimed that everyone agreed with his ideas, he never understood why they were never carried out.

In less than three weeks, Sherman moved his army from Savannah to Columbia at an impressive rate of ten to twelve miles a day, often putting logs on the ground so the army's wagons could travel on the muddy roads. During this time, his men faced only three serious threats: at Rivers Bridge, in Aiken and in Orangeburg. In fact, the weather would prove to be a more serious threat to Sherman in South Carolina than the Confederate army.

On the night of February 16, Hampton and Beauregard informed Columbia's mayor, Thomas Jefferson Goodwyn, that they were going to evacuate military personnel from the city the next morning. Goodwyn had two concerns. The first involved cotton bales piled into the streets of the city. To prevent this valuable resource from falling into the enemy's hands, Confederate officials had intended to take the bales out of the city into the open country to be destroyed, but a lack of time, wagons and animals made that task impossible. Quickly, orders were drawn up stating that the cotton was not to be burned.

The second issue revolved around the large quantity of alcoholic beverages that had been sent to Columbia from Charleston for safekeeping. In 1862, the Confederacy passed a form of prohibition that banned the manufacturing of distilled alcoholic beverages in the hopes that it would lead to increased food production. But the law was flawed; it still allowed citizens to purchase, own, import and consume said beverages. Consequently, the price for beer, liquor and wines increased dramatically to the point where a bottle of Scotch was as good as gold and far more valuable than Confederate currency. Both Hampton and Beauregard declined to address the matter, arguing that because it was civilian property it was out of their jurisdiction.

This last decision proved fateful when the Union soldiers entering Columbia were greeted by slaves, Unionists and escaped prisoners of war offering alcoholic beverages in bottles, jugs, gourds, cups and anything else they could pour liquid into. A quirk in Union military regulations allowed the soldiers to partake of the spirits while on duty, as long as they did not get drunk. However, many of the soldiers had not slept in days and had not

Sherman's Entrance into Columbia. This *Harper's Weekly* illustration shows the general being greeted by intoxicated soldiers. Notice the cotton flying in the air.

eaten in eighteen hours, which intensified the effect of the drinks. Attempts to relieve the drunken troops during the day proved ineffective, as the relief troops got drunk themselves.

At some point in the afternoon, the cotton in the street was set on fire. While it is still debated who lit the cotton, all accounts agree that the cotton-related fires were put out before dusk. After that, Union bayonets sliced the hoses of the local firefighting equipment.

About 7:00 p.m., three rockets were seen in the Columbia sky. The firing of the rockets was a standard military procedure that allowed the different corps to show where they were in relation to one another. By accident or design, this seemed to be a signal that the destruction of Columbia would commence. Witnesses reported seeing hundreds of fires starting all around the city shortly afterward.

The blaze was so bright that one could read a newspaper outdoors, and its glow was seen nearly one hundred miles away. During the inferno, local citizens claimed that every kind of abuse imaginable was committed by the soldiers on the civilian population. Fires continued until about 3:00 a.m., when the winds shifted and started fanning the flames over the burned-out parts of the city. Some witnesses claimed that a bugler on Main Street sounded a horn, which was a signal to stop pillaging and restore order

The Burning of Columbia. This famous *Harper's Weekly* illustration depicts the intersection of Main and Washington Streets during the fire and shows the destruction of city hall and the county courthouse. Notice the dancing soldiers and the frightened women and children in the bottom right of the illustration.

Ruins of Columbia, looking north from the State House. Photographer George Barnard took this famous photograph of Main Street showing the devastation from the fire of February 17, 1865. *From the National Archives.*

immediately. By the next morning, 3,500 soldiers and civilians were arrested, including "officers of nearly every grade." Major General Oliver Otis Howard, commander of the Federal Army of the Tennessee and Sherman's second in command, wrote that hundreds of soldiers were killed in the fire.

About one-third of the city was destroyed during the fire. On Main Street, the commercial center of the town, only the French Consulate miraculously remained. In 1866, property damages were estimated at $30 million, the modern equivalent of $544 million.

According to historian William Gilmore Simms, lost in the fire were:

- 265 dwellings or buildings used as stores and dwellings
- 107 stores
- 40 buildings used as banks, offices, barbershops and stables
- 15 warehouses and train depots
- 19 factories, mills and machine shops
- 7 church buildings
- 4 schools
- 4 printing and engraving plants
- 5 public buildings
- 2 hotels

Several public buildings key to the Confederate cause were deliberately destroyed the next day. Among them were a sword factory, the buildings at the Fair Grounds, a foundry, several railroad depots, armories, the city waterworks and the public gas works. In the process, the Federals destroyed

- 1,000 bales of cotton
- 19 locomotives
- 20 boxcars
- 2 large freight sheds
- 60 sets of mule team harnesses
- 1,000 pounds of trace chains
- 5 tons of railroad machinery
- 650 railroad car wheels
- 2 buildings filled with Confederate stationery
- 25 powder mills (most along the Congaree River)
- an armory
- 6 factories

Emma LeConte took a walk around the city on February 21. To her the city was now an "abomination of desolation." After her tour she wrote, "It is even worse than I thought. The place is literally in ruins. The entire heart of the city is in ashes." She observed that the air in the wrecked city was "frought [*sic*] with sadness and silence." A Union officer wrote, "The city looks more dreary than before, and the destruction more complete. The smoke has cleared away, and the standing chimneys and dried trees look gloomy indeed."

The Federal army left Columbia on February 20, 1865. Sherman was rather pleased with what he and his men had done. He later wrote, "From the moment my army passed Columbia, S.C. the war was ended."

The following re-creates, as close as possible, the route Sherman took into Columbia on February 15–17, 1865. One should allow a full day to follow this tour if you choose to spend time at Riverbanks Zoo.

From the State House, take Assembly Street south to Blossom Street. Turn right on Blossom and continue across the Congaree River. When you cross the river you are in Cayce, and Blossom Street becomes Knox Abbott Drive. Turn left at the second traffic light onto State Street. Continue on State Street for about a mile until you reach Frink Street (SC Highway 2). Turn right and continue for about a mile to Twelfth Street, SC Highway 35.

At Twelfth Street, turn left and go about a mile until you reach Godley Road. Follow the signs for the Congaree Creek Heritage Preserve. Godley Road will end at New State Road. Take a right and follow it until it forks with Old State Road at the boat landing sign. You may wish to stop and read the historical marker about the battle there. Take the right fork onto Old State Road. Follow the paved and dirt road for about a mile until you cross a bridge over a wide creek. Pull off on the side of the road.

1. CONGAREE CREEK

Congaree Creek, or "the Little Congaree River," is a small tributary of the Congaree River. Here archaeologists have found evidence of almost ten thousand years of continuous human habitation. In this area the Congaree Indians, for whom the creek and river are named, once lived. In 1718 Fort Congaree, an Indian trading post, was built in this area. Another nearby outpost, Fort Granby, was the site of several American Revolutionary War battles in 1781.

On February 15, 1865, a mixed Confederate force of dismounted cavalry and infantry, under the command of Major General Matthew C. Butler,

Congaree Creek earthworks. The only major attempt to defend Columbia was made here on February 15, 1865. The site is being developed into a park.

fought the First Division of the Fifteenth Corps of the Federal army, led by Major General Charles Woods. Woods, a future U.S. Supreme Court justice, had what may be the most bizarre nickname of the war: "Susan."

Butler's men defended the creek from behind earthen works that were up to twelve feet in height. Major John Niernsee, State House architect (see #20) who also served in the Confederate army as an engineer, designed this system of defenses, but a shortage of time, men and materials prevented him from finishing his work. The lines went only about one hundred feet, defended by rifles and artillery.

The Confederates tried to delay the Federal advance by burning the wooden bridge over the creek, but miscommunication and wet weather prevented them from fully destroying it, allowing the Federals to save it. After a spirited engagement, the Federals outflanked the Confederates, forcing them to retreat to Columbia. This was the only major attempt to defend the city.

The battle did have one interesting effect. Many of the Union's Fifteenth Corps were upset that Major General Henry Slocum's Army of

Georgia stayed out of the battle, especially since Butler's force was trapped between Woods's and Slocum's troops and could have been destroyed. Though Sherman never shared his thoughts on Slocum's performance, he did decide that the Army of the Tennessee and not the Army of Georgia would have the honor of capturing Columbia, despite Slocum's men being closer to Columbia.

The land surrounding Congaree Creek is full of poisonous snakes and plants, insects and other dangerous animals. This private property has been ceded to the Riverfront Alliance, which is currently developing plans for a public archaeological park on the site. Please do not leave the road and go exploring. Retrace your route to New State Road until you reach the Cayce Boat Landing. Turn into its parking lot.

2. Federal Campsite

Near or on this site, Sherman's men camped for the night. They did not get much rest because the Confederates shelled them from the opposite side of the river, killing one man. This angered Sherman, who mentioned in his memoirs that he considered destroying the city in retaliation. He claimed he kept this thought to himself and later changed his mind. That night Sherman issued Special Orders 26, which read, in part: "General Howard will cross the Saluda and Broad Rivers as near their mouths as possible, occupy Columbia, destroy the public buildings, railroad property, manufacturing and machine shops, but will spare libraries and asylums and private dwellings."

Turn right out of the parking lot and return to Twelfth Street.

3. State Road

The dirt road that leads to Congaree Creek is part of the original State Road, South Carolina's first planned road that went from the coast to the mountains. State Street in Cayce and West Columbia also follows the old road plan. Sherman followed this road for several miles en route to Columbia.

At this point you may wish to take in a side tour and visit the Cayce Historical Museum. Those desiring to visit the museum should continue on Twelfth Street. Shortly after crossing the railroad tracks, you will come to Walter Price Road. Turn left. The next site is up the hill to the right of the Cayce Municipal complex.

4. Cayce Historical Museum

1800 Twelfth Street, Cayce

The museum is housed in a reconstruction of the Cayce House, an eighteenth-century trading post that was passed by Sherman's men as they traveled along the State Road. The museum contains exhibits and artifacts showing how the area has changed in the last two hundred years, including an exhibit on Camp Sorghum (see #7).

For more information about the Cayce Historical Museum, call (803) 796-9020 or visit www.cityofcayce-sc.gov/visiting.

Cayce Historical Museum.

From here you have two choices on how to reach the next site. Those who wish to follow Sherman's route should turn right on Twelfth Street back to Frink Street and turn left. Turn left at State Street, then turn right at Knox Abbot Drive.

Those who desire a more direct route should turn left at Twelfth Street and follow it to Knox Abbott Drive and turn right.

On Knox Abbott Drive, take the first left past Parkland Plaza Shopping Center, Alexander Road. Follow the curvy road until you see the stop sign at Meeting Street. Just before the stop sign, turn right into the parking lot for the Riverfront Park amphitheatre. Go down to the walking path and turn left toward the bridge. Be sure to note the historic markers along the way.

5. GERVAIS STREET BRIDGE

The present bridge is the third one erected on this site. The Confederates destroyed the first one, built in 1827, to prevent its use by Sherman's army. Another one was built in 1870 and lasted until the current one was erected in 1927. Remains of the nineteenth-century structures can be seen on the west bank of the Congaree River north of the current span. Likewise, the remains of the old bridge abutments can be seen in the water north of the current structure when the river is low.

In this area, Union Captain Francis DeGress set up the artillery batteries that shelled the city. It is most likely that the cannonballs that struck the State House were fired from the foot of the nineteenth-century bridge.

DeGress fired into the city because he had seen some cavalrymen and suspected that there were infantry hiding in the city ready to ambush the Federal forces. Sherman knew no such force existed. He ordered DeGress not to fire into the town, except for a few shells at a train depot that was being looted by local citizens. Sherman needed the grain there for his army. DeGress was also allowed three shots at the new State House.

Today, six stars on the west and south sides of the State House mark the spots where the cannonballs found their target. Another ten cannonballs entered the roofless building. Ironically, the building was roofless because a temporary roof might be a fire hazard. One of the cannonballs was located in 1996 while workers were renovating the structure.

Sherman claimed that he had never heard of anyone killed by DeGress's shelling, though local accounts suggest that two people were killed.

Gervais Street Bridge ruins. When the Congaree River is low, the remains of the nineteenth-century structure can be seen to the north of the current bridge.

Return to your car. Turn right from the parking lot. Turn left at Meeting Street and then take the right fork onto Sunset Boulevard (U.S. Highway 378). Drive about a mile until you see the historic marker on your right, just after the Highway 12 underpass. Pull into the parking lot.

6. Shelling of Columbia

One of DeGress's artillery batteries fired into the city from this point. The Prussian-born DeGress was considered one of the best artillerists in the entire Union army.

From the parking lot go to your right to North Lucas Street. Go to the stop sign. Turn right. The large radio towers are on the site of Camp Sorghum.

7. CAMP SORGHUM

Near or on this site was a prisoner-of-war camp where an estimated 1,300 to 1,400 Federal officers were detained in a five-acre open field from October to December 1864. Though the camp was never given an official name, it was generally referred to as "Camp Sorghum," since sorghum molasses was the main food staple of the prisoners. The site was also sometimes referred to as "Yankee City."

The prisoners here had originally been held in Georgia, but when Sherman's army overran that state, they were sent to Charleston. Unfortunately, the officials in Charleston had no place for them and were worried about a possible outbreak of yellow fever. With no warning or authorization, the prisoners were shipped to Columbia. Local officials quickly scouted the countryside to find an adequate place for the prisoners and decided on this location. Two factors that went into choosing this site were the presence of

Camp Sorghum, the infamous prisoner-of-war camp where Federal officers were held, is depicted in this *Harper's Weekly* illustration. Some sources claimed that Columbia was burned in retaliation for Camp Sorghum.

a stream and the belief that the Saluda and Congaree Rivers would prevent escapes. This last point proved to be incorrect.

The camp was not secure; 373 prisoners, almost one-third of the prison population, escaped due to the poor quality of the guards. Mary Chesnut wrote in November 1864, "Squads of Yankee prisoners escape every night." The guards were mostly raw recruits, often teenagers and elderly men, and despite the qualms about their "quality," they were the only ones available. Often the prisoners would follow the Saluda River up to North Carolina, where Union sympathizers would guide them to the Federal lines in Tennessee.

There were never any permanent buildings erected, only about twenty tents. While the prisoners did not suffer as badly as those in the notorious Andersonville, Georgia prison, they were still poorly treated. Food was in short supply for prisoners and guards alike; disease ran rampant.

Most of the men stayed in holes in the ground called she-bangs, covered with leaves, tree limbs or anything else lying around. In December 1864, the remaining prisoners were moved to the South Carolina State Hospital (see #39), an improvement for both the prisoners and their guards. The prisoners were in better shelter and were kept behind a strong brick wall. When Sherman neared Columbia, the prisoners were transferred to Charlotte.

When the Fifteenth Corps headed to the Saluda River, they passed through the remains of the camp. This had a powerful effect on the Federals, as the burrows that the prisoners had dug for shelter were still visible, leading to anger over the sufferings their brother soldiers had endured. Some would later claim that the burning of Columbia was in retaliation for Camp Sorghum. The corps burned what little was left on the site before marching on.

About two hundred escaped prisoners were still in Columbia when Sherman arrived. Having no great love for their captors, they filled the newly arrived troops with fiery talk about why the wrath of the Union should come down on Columbia. This idea became easier to sell as the troops became increasingly inebriated. Nevertheless, even if they had not said a word, the pathetic condition of the ex-POWs would have been enough to fuel the wrath of many in Sherman's army.

On an interesting side note, years after the war, an ex-inmate of Camp Sorghum, Brevet Brigadier General John B. Dennis, became a prison superintendent in Columbia. Another prisoner, Samuel Byers, would gain fame as a writer and would serve as the U.S. ambassador to Switzerland.

At the stop sign in front of the towers, turn right onto Comanche Trail until you come to Laurel Crest Drive. Turn right onto Saluda Trail; then left on North Lucas Street back to Highway 378.

Turn right onto the highway at the traffic light. Continue down the highway until you reach I-26. Take I-26 west about a half mile until you reach I-126. Take I-126 to Columbia until you reach the Greystone Boulevard exit. Turn left off the interstate. The zoo will be on your right. Enter Riverbanks Zoo and Botanical Gardens.

The next three sites are on the property of the zoo. Admission is charged. Call (803) 779-8717 or visit www.riverbanks.org for more information.

Inside the zoo, take the tram from the restaurant area beside the Aquarium and Reptile building. Exit the tram at the entrance to the Botanical Gardens. Enjoy the spectacular floral displays all the way to the back of the gardens. There is a path leading down the hill that is paved, though not smooth. (CAUTION: This is a steep hill and is NOT wheelchair accessible. Those with physical limitations should exercise care.) Benches and handrails are on the steep areas, and steps are nicely spaced along the walkway.

8. SHERMAN'S ROCK

Near the bottom of the hill there is a large boulder on the left, up high, away from the path. This small cave-like formation is called "Sherman's Rock." Local tradition holds that Sherman spent the night of February 16, 1865, under this large boulder. Sherman lends credence to this legend in his *Memoirs*, stating, "I camped near an old prison bivouac."

Until the zoo sealed off this area, this site was a popular picnic area for Columbians.

Continue down the hill to the overlook and housed exhibits.

9. SALUDA FACTORY

Here are the remains of one of the largest textile mills in the world and one of the oldest in South Carolina. In 1834, the Saluda Manufacturing Company was chartered by the General Assembly. The investors built a four-story granite structure with a dam that covered the Saluda River.

Financial problems forced the owners to sell the mill in 1839, setting off a series of ownership changes through the years. In 1855, Colonel James G. Gibbes acquired the property. He renamed the factory the Columbia Cotton

Saluda Factory. Sherman's Fifteenth Corps destroyed the factory on February 16, 1865.

Ruins of the Saluda Factory.

Mill (though the name Saluda Factory stuck). About one thousand people worked eighty looms and thousands of spindles during the war years, with eighteen-foot-diameter wheels generating the power to move the machinery. Originally slaves furnished most of the labor, but during the war years, hired help, mostly female, did the work. An estimated fifty thousand Confederate uniforms were made here.

Gibbes sold the mill in 1862 for half of what he paid for it because he was tired of the "unjust, unkind and un-Christian attacks" he was getting for the high prices the mill charged for goods. While getting only half of one's investment back might not seem like good business sense, it proved to be a fortunate move in the end.

As it happened, the Union Fifteenth Corps came to the door of the mill on February 16. Despite the danger they faced, a number of female employees were in the mill trying to salvage as much of the cloth as possible for their personal use. When informed that they would have to leave the building because it was about to be torched, the women became rather angry and protested that it would leave them unemployed. Their pleas fell on deaf ears. Before the factory was burned, sharpshooters were posted in the windows to deal with potential Confederate snipers.

The factory was rebuilt in 1874, but it was still unprofitable. When it burned down again in 1886, it was not rebuilt. In time, the picturesque ruins became a popular picnic spot for Columbians. In 1898, the ruins were bought by the Columbia Water Power Company, which sold them to South Carolina Electric & Gas in 1911. In the early 1970s, SCE&G leased the land to the zoo for ninety-nine years at a cost of one dollar a year. In 1995, the site was developed and opened to the public.

Be sure to enjoy the displays in the building, which feature drawings from the time of the mill's operation and destruction.

Continue walking down the hill on the path until you emerge from the woods onto the paved road that the tram took you up previously. Immediately to your left is a bridge over the Saluda River.

10. Saluda River Crossing

As you cross the pedestrian bridge over the Saluda River, look to your right. The islands in the river are the ruins of the State Road Bridge that crossed this river in the nineteenth century. The bridge was destroyed by the Confederates to delay Sherman's men. Near where you are standing, Major General John Logan's Fifteenth Corps laid a pontoon bridge over the river and crossed without much incident late in the afternoon of February 16, 1865.

When you are finished visiting the zoo, take a left after you leave the zoo parking lot to Greystone Boulevard north towards Broad River Road. The hill on the opposite side of Interstate 126 from the zoo is the next site.

11. Wheeler's Pickets

On this hill, pickets from Confederate Major General Joseph Wheeler's Cavalry Corps harassed Union troops as they climbed the hill, fighting all the way to the Broad River. It was in this general area that Logan's men camped for the night on February 16, 1865.

Wheeler (1836–1906) was born near Augusta, Georgia, but was raised by relatives in New England. He graduated from West Point in 1859. Despite Wheeler's northern upbringing, he sided with the Confederacy when Georgia seceded.

Major General Joseph Wheeler. Wheeler was one of the Confederate army's top cavalry leaders and one of its most controversial generals. *Courtesy of the Library of Congress.*

From 1862 to 1864, Wheeler served in the Confederate Army of Tennessee, becoming its chief cavalry officer, though ironically, his worst grades at West Point were in cavalry tactics. When Major General J.E.B. Stuart was killed in battle, Wheeler became the Confederate army's ranking cavalry officer. By war's end, he had fought in 127 engagements and had sixteen horses shot under him, but he was wounded only three times.

During Sherman's March to the Sea, Wheeler provided the only serious threat to the Yankees.

In Aiken, Wheeler came close to trapping Sherman's cavalry, led by Major General Judson Kilpatrick, a West Point classmate of Wheeler. Though the trap was sprung prematurely, Wheeler did successfully repel the Union cavalrymen and save the town, the only time that Sherman was stopped in South Carolina.

Wheeler's men had a very unsavory reputation with civilians, who looked upon them "more as a band of highway robbers than as an organized military band," in part because Wheeler's men had not received pay or rations in months, forcing them to beg, borrow and steal to survive.

When the Spanish-American War broke out in 1898, sixty-three-year-old Wheeler volunteered for service. President William McKinley, a Union veteran, named Wheeler a major general of the volunteers. Wheeler served in both Cuba and the Philippines, often unintentionally amusing his troops by referring to Spanish soldiers as "Yankees." In Cuba, he commanded future U.S. President Theodore Roosevelt's Rough Riders at the Battle of San Juan Hill.

Wheeler is one of only two Confederate generals buried in Arlington National Cemetery.

Continue toward Broad River Road and take a right down the hill. Just after crossing the bridge, turn left onto the dirt road. This leads to the parking lot for the north end of the Columbia Canal.

12. BROAD RIVER CROSSING

To the north of the present span stood the Broad River Bridge, a 175-yard-long covered wooden bridge, with two divided lanes.

On the afternoon of February 16, 1865, Wheeler was making preparations to destroy the bridge. Sherman wanted the bridge saved and ordered his men to move as fast as possible to try to save the span. However, Wheeler's men had smothered the Broad River Bridge in tar, turpentine and other flammable materials. Wheeler placed two cavalry brigades and an artillery battery a half mile in front of the bridge to delay the Federal advance.

Wheeler told the battery's commander, Lieutenant Andrew Sea, "to put his guns in position to destroy the bridge" after Wheeler's men had recrossed it. This concerned Sea, who was afraid that "I could not fire on [the Federals] without endangering our own men. If I fired too soon, I might kill some of our men; and if I did not fire soon enough, the Yankees might capture the bridge."

However, the speed and size of the Federal advance forced Wheeler's men to rush back across the bridge. Just before 4:00 p.m., Sea assumed that all of Wheeler's men were across the bridge and signaled his artillerist to fire at the bridge. The bridge was set on fire at its west end and center and was completely destroyed in thirty minutes. One Federal wrote that the bridge "burned so rapidly that the effort to save any part of it was a failure."

Soon, Lieutenant Sea was "greatly distressed" to see that not everyone had crossed it. A member of the rear guard, John Lewis, wrote that they "fully expected that some one would notify us when the bridge was fired." But after defending their position for ten to fifteen minutes, they noticed that the structure was on fire and made a mad dash for the burning structure.

One of the Confederate cavalrymen wrote, "The air was superheated and the smoke was dense and stifling, making it a fearful place through which to run the gauntlet for life. When I went through this fire, I felt as if I almost burned up and as if my eyes were blistered." He covered his face with his hat and ran through fifteen feet of flames. Though he survived, his "hands and face and ears were blistered, my hat scorched and my brow and eyes felt as if they were on fire." Twenty Confederate cavalrymen were so badly burned that they had to be hospitalized.

Wheeler was one of the last men to leave the bridge, and his "hair and the mane of his horse were singed." Two Confederate cavalrymen decided not to risk the bridge and hid in the riverbank's shrubbery and avoided capture. Likewise, a small squad of Confederates decided to move up the river and try to find a crossing, though it would take them a week to rejoin Wheeler's command.

The bridge's destruction meant that Sherman had to erect another pontoon bridge and wait another day to enter the city. That night, Colonel George Stone, commander of the Third Brigade of the First Division of the Fifteenth Corps, made a pontoon boat and crossed the river to the north end of the Columbia Canal, about a half mile above the bridge. Stone's men moved down the canal. He chased away Confederate pickets and protected the Federal army's engineers as they built a pontoon bridge for the rest of the corps to cross. The pontoons were placed to the north of the modern bridge.

To learn more on the nineteenth-century bridge's history and the investigation into its exact location, visit www.dobrinkman.net/bridge.

To walk to the site via the Columbia Canal trail, follow the path starting at the canal's north end and head south toward the city. Be sure to take note of the informational signs along the trail.

When you return to Broad River Road, turn left to continue the tour. Up the hill from the bridge, the road forks. Take the right fork, River Drive. Drive a half mile until you see Burning Bush Missionary Baptist Church on your right at the southwest corner of River Drive and Beaufort Street.

13. Surrender Monument

This boulder marks the spot where Mayor Thomas Goodwyn formally surrendered the city to Colonel Stone, who was moving toward the city after securing the river crossing.

Goodwyn asked for terms but was told that surrender had to be unconditional. After agreeing to this, he produced a letter to Sherman:

> *The Confederate forces having evacuated Columbia, I deem it my duty, as Mayor and representative of the city, to ask for its citizens the treatment accorded by the usages of civilized warfare. I therefore respectfully request that you will send a sufficient guard in advance of the army to maintain order in the city and protect the persons and property of the citizens.*

Mayor Thomas Goodwyn. The planter and physician turned politician surrendered the city to Sherman.

Surrender Monument. Where the city of Columbia was officially surrendered to the Union army.

Stone quickly sent a messenger to inform Sherman, who was waiting for the pontoon bridge to be finished over the Broad River. He was amusing himself by whittling on a stick while sitting on a log with General Howard. The messenger informed the generals that the city was surrendered and asked if there were any orders. The letter from the mayor was also passed on to Sherman, who replied, "General Howard...had his orders, to let Col. Stone go on into the city, and that we would follow as soon as the bridge was ready." Sherman gave no written acknowledgment of having received the mayor's letter.

This monument was erected in 1914. A Union scout who witnessed the surrender helped in the placement of the marker.

From the church, continue down River Drive until it merges with North Main Street.

At this point you might want to take a slight detour and visit the following two sites. To get to the first one, turn left on North Main Street and then take the first right onto Geiger Street. Otherwise, turn right on North Main Street and continue toward Elmwood Avenue and site #16.

14. Confederate Cemetery

Located in the center of a park at the intersection of Geiger and Cardinal Streets.

This small cemetery contains the graves of several Confederate veterans and their families, as well as the remains of patients from the nearby State Hospital.

Retrace your route on Geiger Street until you come to Marion Street. Turn left and then turn left on Confederate Avenue. Park your car before you get to Bull Street. The monument is on your left in an empty lot.

15. Site of the Confederate Soldiers Home

Monument located at the northwest corner of Confederate Avenue and Bull Street.

This monument commemorates the Confederate Soldiers Home, which was located at 1417 Confederate Avenue. Created by an act of the legislature in 1908, after years of lobbying by the United Confederate Veterans and the United Daughters of the Confederacy, this facility housed veterans of the Confederate military who were either poor or in poor health. The home, then on the outskirts of town, was donated for this purpose.

The house was a large, one-story frame structure with gabled roofs and a long porch with four tall columns at the entranceway. Unfortunately, the home was generally underfunded, so to supplement their food supply, the veterans farmed twenty acres of land donated by the State Hospital.

In 1925, the wives and widows of Confederate soldiers and sailors were allowed to reside here. Later acts allowed sisters, daughters and nieces of veterans to reside here, too.

In the 1920s, Captain W.H. Stuart, superintendent of the home, started a drive to erect a monument at Elmwood Cemetery to the memory of those who died at the home. With the blessing of government officials and residents, Stuart saved enough money from the home's 1925 appropriations to have the marker made. It was dedicated on Confederate Memorial Day, May 10, 1926, with sixty names inscribed on it.

Sadly, Captain Stuart was not present to see his dream come true. He had died on March 19. Later, at the suggestion of a speaker at the dedication, Captain Stuart's name was etched on the monument he labored so long to have erected. The names of eleven other residents of the home were later added.

The home's last veteran died here in 1941. Due to a declining enrollment, the home was closed in 1957. At the time, there were twenty residents who were relocated to boarding facilities. Though the building no longer remains, its legacy lives on; Confederate Avenue was named for the home.

Turn your car around and return to North Main Street and turn left. The next site is located about a half mile away at the corner of Main Street and Elmwood Avenue.

16. "Cotton Town"

Because most of the city's cotton warehouses were located in this area, this part of Columbia became known as "Cotton Town." When Sherman neared, cotton was stacked outdoors in this area awaiting transportation away from the city for destruction so it would not fall into Union hands. According to some accounts, the fire that swept through Columbia started in this area.

Even though it has been years since cotton was stored or sold in this area, Cotton Town is still used as the name for the residential area bounded by Main, Elmwood, Bull and Grace Streets.

Continue south on Main Street for about a mile until you reach the Barringer Building at 1338 Main Street, on the southeast corner of Main and Washington Streets.

17. Court House Square/City Hall

The third Richland County courthouse was located here. Records from across the state were stored here for safekeeping. Federal troops stacked their arms in this area after entering the city. Sherman claimed that the fire started in this vicinity.

Across the street on the southwest corner of Main and Washington was Columbia's first city hall. The Union soldiers from the Thirty-second Illinois Regiment who first raised the Union flag over this building were locked in its tower so no one could remove their banner. However, when the men in the tower got drunk and started firing their guns into the street, they were freed. Both buildings were destroyed in the fire.

Nearby was the home of a successful local merchant named Jacob Feaster. His wife, Amelia, was one of Columbia's most notorious women. Originally from Philadelphia, Mrs. Feaster was widowed three times before she was in her thirties. She met Jacob while settling the estate of her third husband, and they were soon married.

Amelia had a teenage daughter from a previous marriage named Marie Boozer. Described by all who saw her as a very beautiful woman, she was notorious for her vanity. Amelia was a "very smart woman and not over-scrupulous" and was hell-bent on climbing the social ladder by using Marie's charms as her way to the top.

When the war started, Amelia made no secret of her pro-Union views, which eroded her marriage. She aided and hid Union spies in her house and helped Federal prisoners escape. According to local legend, Amelia bragged to Sherman in person about her assistance to the Federal cause. She also told the general that her husband's warehouse contained supplies that the Federals could use. In appreciation for her assistance, Sherman gave Mrs. Feaster two horses for her carriage.

When Sherman left Columbia, Amelia, Marie and another daughter joined the hundreds of Unionist refugees who accompanied Sherman's army into North Carolina. Thanks to their feminine charms, the ladies became popular with any soldier with whom they came in contact. Some troops even "borrowed" a nicer carriage for the women to ride more comfortably.

Upon their arrival in Fayetteville, North Carolina, the ladies took a boat to New York and never returned to the Palmetto State. In December 1865, Amelia asked the mayor of Columbia to issue a certificate declaring Jacob Feaster dead so she could collect some money. He declined since Mr. Feaster was still alive. Amelia died in 1870 at the young age of forty-five, while her "dead" husband outlived her by twenty-five years.

Marie was the subject of gossip and legends for decades and was written about more than some Civil War generals. The federally funded *WPA Guide to the Palmetto State*, published in 1941, accurately called Boozer "a dubious symbol of Yankee victory" who "drew down upon herself the wrath of the citizens."

Unfortunately, the book also published as fact one of the typical lies and half-truths that spread about her, claiming that she married a Union officer in North Carolina. It further asserted that she traveled with a friend of Louis Napoleon (Napoleon III), Cora Pearl, and was linked to a scandal involving Russian jewels. It also said that Marie married a Japanese nobleman "who because of her infidelities…had her beheaded."

In reality, Marie married a wealthy New York oil merchant but left him after he cheated on her. After her divorce, she moved to France and married the Count de Pourtales, a member of the French Foreign Service, with whom she had a happy marriage. Boozer died at her husband's villa near Florence, Italy, in January 1908, having suffered from several years of ill health and depression.

Marie's life was the subject of two historical novels: *Another Jezebel: A Yankee Spy in South Carolina* by Neil S. Graydon and Elizabeth Boatwright Coker's *La Belle: A Novel Based on the Life of the Notorious Southern Belle, Marie Boozer.*

The next site is visible from this spot; just look to the west, behind the brown skyscraper.

18. City Jail Site

Northeast corner of Washington and Assembly Streets

One of the few things that Confederate, civilian and Federal accounts of the destruction of Columbia agree upon is that sometime early in the day of February 17, persons unknown set fire to the jail and released all the prisoners. This act angered many Union officers, some of whom later claimed that the escapees played a major role in the fire that night.

Continue one block down Main Street.

19. Site of Beauregard's Headquarters

Stop at 1301 Main Street, the Rodeway Inn on the northwest corner of Main and Lady Streets.

Here stood T.S. Nickerson's Congaree House Hotel, sometimes referred to as Nickerson's Hotel. During the war, it was the scene of many activities. In 1862, while General James and Mary Chesnut stayed here, Mrs. Chesnut wrote some of her famous diary. Later, in 1865, General Beauregard set up his headquarters here. From here he issued the orders to evacuate Columbia.

Confederates were not the only ones to appreciate its accommodations. A large number of Federal officers checked into the hotel when the city was occupied. Unfortunately for them, the hotel was destroyed in the fire. After the war, Nickerson would reestablish his hotel in the vacant buildings of Columbia College on Hampton Street, which he leased until 1872.

Continue one block. The State House is in the center of Main Street.

20. STATE HOUSE

1100 Gervais Street

The State House is one of only two surviving pre–Civil War structures on Main Street, which was originally called Richardson Street. Construction began in 1854, but work was halted when the foundation failed. The next year, the legislature hired John R. Niernsee of Baltimore to design and build the present facility. Work began anew in 1856, and by 1865, the exterior walls were mostly finished, though the building lacked a roof and interiors.

Despite rumors that Sherman's men wanted to blow it up, Sherman thought the structure was "handsome" and decided to spare it. He was not alone; many Federal soldiers praised the building's appearance. The Federals

Raising the Stars and Stripes over the State House. This illustration from *Frank Leslie's Illustrated Newspaper* also shows how much work remained to be done on the structure in 1865.

scarred the building. The west and south sides bear six stars marking where cannonballs hit it. Also on the southwest corner, the flames of the burning wooden State House damaged some of the trim.

Unerected columns were damaged or destroyed, as were wrought iron, marble and granite. Statues and busts intended for the building were destroyed, and two monuments were damaged. In 1865, Niernsee estimated the loss of materials at $1 million, or $13.6 million in today's dollars.

In the 1870s, a temporary roof was put on the building, but it was not until 1903 that the building was proclaimed "finished" thanks to politics and inadequate funding. Further complicating the work was the loss of all the building's architectural plans and drawings in the fire.

The building's current appearance is different from Niernsee's original vision. The most noticeable variation is a dome instead of a tower over the structure. Since its "completion," the State House has been renovated several times. The most recent and intensive lasted from 1995 to 1998, when the inside of the building was remodeled to bring the structure into the twenty-first century and give the interior a more unified, nineteenth-century look. However, the destruction of the building's plans delayed completion for six months and added millions of dollars to its cost.

Inside the State House are numerous portraits of Confederate leaders, as well as memorials to individuals and military units that played a part in the War Between the States.

On the grounds of the State House are several monuments with Civil War connections. Start on the front steps and walk counterclockwise around the building to see each.

A. Washington's Statue

This life-size statue of George Washington faces north. Antoine Houdon carved the original in 1796 for the State of Virginia. South Carolina acquired this bronze copy in 1858.

During Sherman's occupation of Columbia, soldiers threw objects at the statue and broke off the lower portion of the walking stick. After the war, it was repaired but was removed by local citizens who wanted to show the Yankees in their "true light." The lower portion is now on display at the South Carolina Confederate Relic Room and Military Museum (see #60).

When you look at Main Street from the statue, you are viewing downtown Columbia from almost the same position as the famous 1865 photo taken by George N. Barnard, the official photographer for the United States

Statue of George Washington. Almost 150 years later, the walking cane remains broken.

Army, Chief Engineer's Office, Division of the Mississippi. He followed Sherman from Georgia through the Carolinas photographing the devastation left behind. In 1866, he published an album of sixty-one photographs called *Photographic Views of Sherman's Campaign*.

B. Confederate Monument

Walk toward Gervais Street to view the official state memorial to the Confederate soldiers of South Carolina. The marble monument stands forty feet high, with a seven-foot-three-inch-tall soldier on the top. Though the soldier is attired like a private, his face resembles General Stephen Elliott, a native of Beaufort, South Carolina, who was in charge of Fort Sumter in 1863.

In 1869, a group of local women organized the Monument Association. Three years later, they purchased a spot on Arsenal Hill around Sydney Park. In July 1873, they hired the Kentucky firm of Muldoon, Walton and Cobb, which specialized in tombstones and memorial statues, to create the monument. The association paid $10,000 for the monument, while Judge John S. Green donated the granite base.

When quicksand was discovered under the soil, the granite base was relocated to a donated lot at Elmwood Cemetery. When the crated monument arrived in September 1875, the association still owed $5,000, so the monument remained crated up at the cemetery for three years.

When Reconstruction ended in 1876, the Monument Association appealed to the state legislature for help. The legislature not only approved the placing of the monument on the grounds of the State House but also agreed to pay the cost of transporting and erecting the memorial.

On March 27, 1879, the monument was dedicated in front of the east wing of the State House, witnessed by a crowd of fifteen thousand spectators. General James Preston, in one of his last public appearances, was the keynote speaker.

Three years later, a bolt of lightning struck the monument, destroying the soldier's head. Fears that the iron roof of the State House might attract lightning led to the monument being moved to its present location on a pedestal that was eighteen inches higher, while a new soldier was put atop the monument.

C. The Site of the Old State House

Go west to the Assembly Street side of the building, to the small granite monument commemorating the second South Carolina State House. The first one still stands at the corner of Broad and Meeting Streets in Charleston. According to tradition, the second State House's architect was James Hoban of Charleston, who also designed the White House. According to eyewitnesses and the few surviving illustrations, the two buildings resembled each other.

This *Harper's Weekly* illustration shows the "Stars and Stripes" being flown over the South Carolina State House by Iowa troops shortly after Sherman took Columbia.

Hoban's wooden State House had a brick raised basement that contained offices and a floor above where the Senate and the House each had their own chambers. The small frame building was cheaply made and constantly needed repairs. One Federal soldier described it as "dingy and forbidding." Goats roamed in the basement. The building's small size and concerns that it was a fire hazard led to the construction of the current State House.

In January 1865, to raise funds for the war effort, the Great Bazaar was held in the old State House, featuring booths from all of the Confederate States, except the "split states" of Missouri and Kentucky. Columbians ran some booths because Union occupation prevented representatives of some states from attending.

Because of inflation, items sold for staggering prices. A slice of cake cost $2, and a small cake fetched $75. Imported wax dolls were raffled from $500 to $2,000. Originally, the bazaar was to last two weeks, but Sherman's approach closed it after only a few days. According to some accounts, the bazaar raised an impressive $350,000, but some questioned the amount raised and where it was spent.

Shortly after occupying Columbia, Federal troops broke into the old State House, shot a portrait of Confederate President Jefferson Davis and threw inkwells and spittoons at a bust of former U.S. Vice President John C. Calhoun. A mock session of the legislature was held in the Senate chambers where the "delegates" voted to censure Calhoun. They then voted to repeal the Ordinance of Secession and, after a rousing version of "John Brown," voted to adjourn to reassemble in Raleigh, North Carolina.

The building was destroyed in the fire of February 17, 1865. Lost in the destruction of this building was the State Library with the architectural plans and drawings of the new State House, papers and artifacts of John C. Calhoun, a bust of President Andrew Jackson, records from the colonial era and twenty-five thousand "choice volumes" of books.

Miss Emma LeConte viewed the remains of the State House with great sadness. "I paused to gaze on the ruins," she wrote, "only the foundations and chimneys—and to recall the brilliant scene enacted there one short month ago. And I compared that scene with its beauty, gayety and festivity—the halls so elaborately decorated, the surging throng—with this."

D. Palmetto Regiment Monument

The oldest monument on the State House grounds is right next to the old State House monument. This cast-iron monument honors the Palmetto Regiment of the Mexican-American War. Their regimental flag, an early version of the present-day South Carolina state flag, was the first American flag flown over Mexico City after its capture by U.S. forces in 1847. The regiment's commander, Colonel Pierce M. Butler, died during the capital's capture.

Christopher Werner of Charleston cast the palmetto tree about 1852. The state legislature bought it in 1856 for $5,000 and commissioned Werner to make plaques naming those who died from the regiment. It was placed in front of the State House.

During the 1865 occupation of Columbia, a Federal solider tried to tear some of the names off the monument. This solider ignored the warnings of his companions who had served with the regiment not to do it. When he ignored their warning, they seized the vandal and proceeded to beat him for committing "a sacrilegious crime." After this incident, the monument seems to have been guarded for the duration of the occupation, as a contemporary sketch shows two of Sherman's men on guard duty at the memorial.

In 1875, a tornado tipped over the monument, and it lay on the ground for three years. In 1878, it was repaired at a cost of $2,000 and placed on the west side of the capital. In the 1970s, it was moved to its present location, near its 1865 location. The monument has been featured in *Ripley's Believe It or Not* because birds have made nests in it.

E. Women of the Confederacy Monument

Go to the south side of the building and then a block south to where Main Street meets Pendleton Street. Here is one of three monuments on the State House grounds designed by Frederick W. Ruckstull, one of the most famous sculptors of his day.

At the 1896 United Confederate Veterans (UCV) convention in Richmond, Virginia, the delegates endorsed erecting memorials to the women who maintained the homefront and supported the war effort. The next year, the South Carolina Division of the UCV began this project.

However, the idea languished until 1906, when General C. Irvine Walker revived and started pushing the idea. Three years later, the legislature created a commission to erect the monument with General Walker as its chairman. The commission raised $21,000 from the public and an additional $7,500 from the legislature. With money in hand, they commissioned Ruckstull to design the memorial.

A cofounder of the National Sculpture Society, Ruckstall won numerous awards for his work in the United States and Europe. His seven-foot, two-

Women of the Confederacy Monument.

inch marble statue of Senator John C. Calhoun represents South Carolina in Statuary Hall in the U.S. Capitol.

This fourteen-foot-tall bronze monument is one of the most beautiful and unique monuments to the Confederate cause found anywhere. When dedicated in 1912, it stood in front of the State House steps on the south side of the building, jutting into Senate Street, which was then opened to traffic. This created a traffic hazard, so it was relocated to the corner of Sumter and Gervais Streets. In 1969, it was moved to its present location.

F. Wade Hampton III Monument

Turn back toward the State House and look to the right to see the equestrian statue to South Carolina's greatest Confederate warrior, Lieutenant General Wade Hampton III. Hampton was born in Charleston in 1818 but was raised and educated in Columbia. Before the war, Hampton's family was one of the richest in America and the South's largest landowners.

Hampton was an outstanding swordsman and an excellent pistol shot. He is said to have personally killed more men in battle than any other general during the war. When once asked how many he had killed, Hampton replied, "Eleven, two with my sword and nine with my pistol." This total did not include two men he killed at Trevilian Station, Virginia, because "they were running."

When the war started, Hampton used his own funds to outfit "Hampton's Legion," an elite military unit of infantry, cavalry and artillery companies, and he served as its colonel. Despite limited formal training, Hampton was a natural military leader. Douglas Freeman wrote in *Lee's Lieutenants*, "[Hampton] may not have possessed military genius, but he had the nearest approach to it." Fearless in battle, Hampton was wounded seven times, receiving two head cuts and shrapnel in the body on the third day of Gettysburg alone.

Hampton served as Major General J.E.B. Stuart's senior division commander in the Army of Northern Virginia's cavalry. When Stuart was killed in battle in 1864, Hampton was named his successor.

Hampton was sent to South Carolina in January 1865 when Major General Matthew C. Butler's cavalry division was sent to the Palmetto State to find new men and mounts. Hampton would boost morale in the state but, more importantly, make sure that Butler's cavalry was not absorbed into Major General Joseph Wheeler's cavalry corps.

Hampton's orders were vague. "My only duty in South Carolina was to assist in putting Butler's Division in the field and that I had no active command in South Carolina on my arrival there," he later wrote, adding that he was nothing more than a "volunteer" on Beauregard's staff.

On February 16, 1865, Hampton was promoted to lieutenant general, making him the ranking cavalry officer in the entire Confederate army for the duration of the war. This promotion was initiated by General Beauregard out of disgust with the complaints he was receiving about how Wheeler handled his corps and how unruly his men were to civilians. Although Wheeler publicly supported Hampton, Wheeler's men came close to mutiny.

Hampton evacuated the city the next day and led his cavalry into North Carolina, where he drew up the battle plans for the Battle of Bentonville. He left the Confederate army prior to General Joseph Johnson's surrender at Durham Station, North Carolina, in order to join the fleeing Jefferson Davis and try to continue the war from Texas. However, poor health and exhaustion forced him to abandon this plan after joining family members in York, South Carolina.

The war left Hampton destitute. He never regained his fortune and was dependent on government salaries and goodwill for the rest of his days. He did enjoy political success as governor of South Carolina (1876–79), U.S. senator (1879–91) and U.S. railroad commissioner (1893–99). He was also a popular speaker and a national officer of the United Confederate Veterans. He died in Columbia in 1902. Over twenty thousand people paid their final respects to him.

Within a week of Hampton's death, the Wade Hampton Camp of the United Confederate Veterans started an initiative to honor the former general. This movement was aided by the United Daughters of the Confederacy. In 1903, the legislature approved $20,000 toward a statue, providing the people of South Carolina raised $10,000 themselves. In 1904, the Wade Hampton Monument Commission was created by the legislature, which hired Ruckstull without consideration of any other sculptors.

The monument was unveiled on November 20, 1906. Ten to twenty thousand people gathered for the unveiling. General Butler gave a one-hour address on the life of his comrade in arms. Originally located on the east side of the State House, the monument was moved to its present location in front of the Wade Hampton office building in 1969.

The bronze statue, the only equestrian monument in South Carolina, stands fifteen and a half feet tall and sits on a thirteen-foot base of granite from South Carolina and France. The statue was cast in Paris, and Ruckstull himself accompanied it from Paris to Columbia. The monument faces the north so that Hampton might gaze upon the route by which Sherman entered the city. Its total cost was $30,000. Critics, including the *New York Times*, gave it high praise as a work of art, while Ruckstull felt it was his finest sculpture. He was later commissioned to carve a marble seven-foot, two-inch statue of the South Carolina leader that was placed in the U.S. Capital building in 1929.

G. African American History Monument

In 1996, State Senators Glenn McConnell, a white Republican, and Darryl Jackson, an African American Democrat, successfully passed legislation authorizing this monument. Designed by Ed Dwight of Denver, Colorado, the $1.1 million bronze and granite monument, paid for by private donations, was dedicated in March 2001. Standing two stories high and twenty-five feet wide, it is the first monument to African American history placed on the grounds of a state capital.

The panel closest to the left of center depicts African American troops from the First South Carolina Regiment who fought for the Union during the war. Based out of Hilton Head, they saw action along the lower South Carolina coast during the war.

For more information on the State House, its grounds or tours of the building call (803) 734-2430 or visit www.scstatehouse.gov/studentpage/tour.htm.

Go east on Gervais Street and then left onto Sumter Street. On the northwest corner of Sumter and Gervais, where the modern South Carolina State Supreme Court Building now sits, is the site of the home of Mayor Thomas Jefferson Goodwyn. Proceed north to Blanding Street. Turn right and take Blanding Street west until you reach Harden Street.

Detail from the African American History Monument. This panel depicts the Union army's First South Carolina Colored Regiment.

You will pass by Logan's headquarters—the Hampton-Preston House (see #34). Benedict College will be in front of you. Notice the railroad tracks across Blanding, which follow the same route as in 1865. This is also the route Confederates used to evacuate the city.

21. Site of the Charlotte Train Depot and Fifteenth Corps Camps

The Charlotte and South Carolina Railroad was the last functioning rail line out of the city. A scene of chaotic activity ensued as Confederate officials desperately tried to evacuate government property from here, but the lack of cars and organization resulted in very little being saved.

When Butler's men left the city, they burned the depot, one of the last acts of the Confederate government in the city. As Butler's men left the city, desperate women cried out to them, "Don't leave us! You can't leave us here!" At the time Sherman entered Columbia, there were virtually no men in the city. One writer has estimated that the ratio of men to women was one to forty in a city with a population of twelve to fourteen thousand, while another historian has estimated that only five hundred men were in the town.

Near where Benedict College now stands, the Second Division, Fifteenth Corps, commanded by Major General William Hazen, camped. Hazen was one of the Union army's best division commanders.

To your left, down the hill, is where Brigadier General Charles Woods's First Division, Fifteenth Corps, was camped. His division was the first Federal unit in Columbia.

Turn right on Harden Street and continue for three miles until you come to Blossom Street in the Five Points area.

22. Five Points

In this area, the Third Division of the Fifteenth Corps, commanded by Brigadier General John Smith, camped. Today it is a popular shopping and dining area.

Turn right on Blossom Street and drive one mile until you come to the second traffic light at Pickens Street. Turn left on Pickens and drive up the hill. On your left at the foot of the hill is Maxcy Gregg Park (circa 1911). Named for the Columbia native, it is the only park in the city named for a Confederate official (see site #38).

As you pass through the first traffic light on Wheat Street, look to your right. In the parking lot by the University of South Carolina's Sol Blott Physical Education Center, on Wheat Street, is a historic marker commemorating the site of the home of Confederate Brigadier General Adley Gladden. Gladden served in the Mexican-American War and was a city postmaster. He died at the Battle of Shiloh in 1862. Go to the top of the hill to the American Legion building on your left.

23. Wheeler Hill

South Pickens Street between Blossom and Heyward Streets

In this area, the Federal Fourth Division of the Fifteenth Corps, commanded by Brigadier General Giles A. Smith, was camped.

This concludes Sherman's route into Columbia.

PART TWO

University of South Carolina Old Campus Area

This section encompasses the area south of Gervais Street between Sumter and Barnwell Streets in downtown Columbia

24. Trinity Episcopal Cathedral

1100 Sumter Street on the corner of Gervais and Sumter Streets

Trinity's congregation was first organized in 1812. Two years later, its members were meeting in a frame church that, according to tradition, was located where a large oak now stands in the cemetery. The present Gothic Revival structure dates from 1846 and is a replica of Yorkminister Cathedral in York, England.

During the Civil War, the iron spires on the top of the church were melted down to make cannonballs for the Confederate army. Prior to Sherman's arrival, the church's stained-glass windows were removed for safekeeping. Legend holds that large papier-mâché crosses were placed on the church to disguise it as a Catholic church because Sherman's men allegedly targeted Episcopal churches since many Confederate leaders were Episcopalian.

Though the chapel escaped serious damage, the parsonage, Sunday school buildings and parish records were destroyed. During the night of the fire, the church's minister, Reverend Peter Shand, his wife and a servant went to the church to retrieve a trunk that contained the communion plate as well as some of the minister's old sermons. They were walking with it

Trinity Episcopal Cathedral. Tradition states that disguising itself as a Catholic church spared the church from destruction.

when five soldiers surrounded the party and demanded that the trunk be put down and its contents disclosed.

Reverend Shand complied. "They then demanded the key," Shand later recalled, "but, I not having it, they proceeded in efforts to break the lock. While four of them were thus engaged, the fifth seized me with his left hand by the collar, and, presenting a pistol to my breast with his right, he demanded of me my watch. I had it not about me." The soldier's comrades, "finding it impracticable to force open the lock, took up the trunk and carried it away." Though the reverend never retrieved the communion plates, he did recover some of his sermons.

Inside the chapel are furnishings donated to the church by the Hampton and Preston families. A plaque on the wall is dedicated to the church members who died for the Confederacy, the oldest being only thirty-four.

The cemetery is one of the most historic in the state. Three Confederate generals, Wade Hampton III, Ellison Capers and the unusually named

States Rights Gist, are buried in the cemetery. Also buried there is Henry Timord, "Poet Laureate of the Confederacy." Under the large tree, called "Governor's Oak," lie the remains of five South Carolina governors.

Other notable persons in the cemetery include Brigadier General Wade Hampton, a hero of the American Revolution and the War of 1812; Wade Hampton II, a prominent antebellum politician and father of the Confederate general; Thomas Cooper, second president of South Carolina College (the modern University of South Carolina) and an early advocate of secession; and James Byrnes, Franklin Roosevelt's "assistant president," a former U.S. senator, Supreme Court justice, secretary of state and South Carolina governor.

The cemetery is open daily during daylight hours. For information on tours of the sanctuary, call (803) 771-7300 or visit www.trinitysc.org.

25. Birthplace of Maxcy Gregg

The historic marker is located on the southeast corner of Senate and Sumter Streets

On this spot was the birthplace of Brigadier General Maxcy Gregg, the only Confederate general born in Columbia. Gregg was born here on August 1, 1814 (though the marker says 1815). Gregg would attend South Carolina College and study law with his father. For more on the general, see site #38.

26. South Carolina College (the University of South Carolina)

900 and 800 blocks of Sumter Street, between Pendleton and Greene Streets

Founded in 1801, South Carolina College was one of the nation's premier institutes of higher learning. Secession was a popular subject among professors and students, being debated frequently during the antebellum era. Proponents of secession almost always won, but the students were not all talk. When the war broke out, the then all-male student body formed a cadet corps with arms provided by the state and joined the Confederate army.

According to one alumnus, everyone who had ever attended the college and "who [was] physically able did service in the army of the Confederacy," including the entire student body who left the school to serve in the Confederate army. An estimated 150 to 160 South Carolina College alumni died serving the Confederacy; 16 former students became brigadier generals in the Confederate army, while 3 others served as major generals. The lone lieutenant general was Wade Hampton III, whose grandfather was one of the original members of the school's board of trustees.

The students' exodus forced the school to close in 1862. The facilities were leased to the Confederate government as a hospital. Unfortunately, the CSA government was not a good tenant. The school and Confederate officials spent two years haggling over the terms and conditions of the lease. Finally, in September 1864, the two parties settled for $60,660. However, by December 1864, the school had still not received the first payment from the Confederate government. At the time, Richmond officials promised to pay as soon as money was available. However, the war ended with the Confederate States still owing the school the full amount.

The school served as a busy hospital, with over three thousand soldiers receiving treatment. It was said that every table and bench on campus was used as an operating table. Despite the volume, it was considered one of the best Confederate military hospitals.

When Sherman arrived, a yellow flag flew over the Horseshoe designating the facility as a hospital, which by military etiquette meant that the site was not to be molested. Furthermore, the hospital had both Confederate and Federal patients, a factor that played into the survival of the school. In addition, some Confederate medical personnel volunteered to remain behind to help tend to the sick and injured.

Though a detachment of guards assigned to the campus had spared the school from vandalism during the chaos of February 17, sparks from the inferno were carried by the strong winds to the rooftops of the campus buildings. Thanks to the efforts of the guards and the hospital staff, the fires were contained before any serious damage was done. But it was a constant battle until the winds died down about 4:00 a.m.

While the fires were fought, the patients had to fend for themselves. Many of them panicked at the thought of being burned alive and literally crawled on their hands and knees or, in some cases, hands and elbows, to get out of the buildings They joined many local residents who were trying to find relative safety. About twenty patients died from exposure while lying outside in the cold February night air.

There was little rest for the weary on the morning of the eighteenth. Between 6:00 and 8:00 a.m., about 150 "drunken cavalry" assailed the gates of campus, threatening to burn the school. When the officer in charge of the hospital's guards became worried that the mob at the gate would overwhelm his men, a surgeon and two professors hurried to see General Howard, whose headquarters was next to the campus. Howard ordered Colonel Stone to go immediately to the college and defuse the situation. With a revolver in his hand, Colonel Stone went to the campus and disbanded the troublemakers.

The campus reopened in 1865, but financial and political instability plagued the school for years, resulting in another closing in 1877. It reopened in 1880 and has been in operation ever since. From 1880 to 1882, William Porcher Miles, designer of the famous Confederate battle flag, often called the "Southern Cross," served as the school's president. During the Civil War, he chaired the Confederate House Military Affairs Committee.

In the center of the Horseshoe is Robert Mills's prewar monument to Jonathan Maxcy, the first president of the school. Mills (1781–1855) was a Charleston native who studied architecture under Thomas Jefferson and James Hoban. Mills was the federal architect of the United States for seven presidents. Among his most famous works are the U.S. Treasury Building and the Washington Monument. Mills also designed numerous buildings for the State of South Carolina. Many of his state projects and some private commissions can still be seen in Columbia.

Today, eleven of the original twelve campus buildings make up the area called the "Horseshoe." The twelfth one was torn down in the 1930s to make way for a new library that is now the McKissick Museum.

Except for the McKissick Museum and the South Caroliniana Library, the buildings on the Horseshoe are used for classrooms, offices or living quarters and are not open to the general public.

A. The South Caroliniana Library

Built in 1840, this was the first separate university library building in America. Designed by Robert Mills, the interior retains much of its original character. The main reading room on the second floor is a replica of the original Library of Congress reading room designed by Charles Bulfinch. On the wall next to the staircase is an antebellum marble plaque honoring Congressman Preston Brooks, whose attack on U.S. Senator Charles Sumner of Massachusetts with a walking stick in the U.S. Senate Chamber furthered regional tensions.

More important to historians is the large number of manuscripts and published material relating to the history of South Carolina. Among

The South Caroliniana Library. One of the few buildings on the Horseshoe to retain much of its original interiors, the library contains an invaluable collection of books, manuscripts and photographs relating to the Civil War.

the library's holdings are the Hampton Family Papers, Mayor Thomas Goodwyn's note to Sherman surrendering Columbia and some of the original diaries of Mary Chesnut.

The South Caroliniana Library is open to the public. Call (803) 777-3131 or visit www.sc.edu/library/socar for hours of operation.

B. Elliott College

This 1837 building was used as a hospital during the war.

C. Harper College

Built in 1848, the top floor was the meeting room of the Euphradian Society, a college debate and literary society whose membership included Thomas Jefferson and Daniel Webster. On the eve of the war, it expelled one member, Francis Lieber, a renowned and distinguished professor who opposed secession and supported Lincoln. Because of his views, Lieber was forced to resign his position and went to Columbia University in New York. After voting to expel the professor, the Euphradians sent his portrait back to the artist who painted it and then threw a bust of him out the window.

During the Federal occupation of Columbia during Reconstruction, four rooms of the building were used as a Federal military prison.

D. Faculty House

Built in 1813, this building housed the school's professors. During its renovation in the late 1970s, slave quarters were discovered in the attic of the house. Unfortunately, they had to be destroyed to make way for equipment and ductwork to bring the building up to twentieth-century standards. However, the quarters were heavily photographed and documented before their destruction.

E. DeSaussure College

Built in 1809, this building was used extensively as a hospital. After the burning of the city, some refugees were housed in its wings.

At the top of the Horseshoe was the original President's House, which was used as an officers' hospital. Many Confederate and Union soldiers who died on the campus were buried behind it (near where McKissick now stands). Later, their bodies were removed and taken to Elmwood Cemetery (see #45).

The McKissick Museum is open to the public. Call (803) 777-7251 or visit www.cas.sc.edu/mcks for more information.

F. Rutledge College

Located on the top of the south side of the Horseshoe, it is the oldest building on the campus, built in 1805. The school's chapel is located in this building. Originally, the building appearance mirrored DeSaussure College, but its façade was altered after an 1855 fire that severely damaged it.

Rutledge College. The oldest building on campus was used as a hospital during the Civil War.

During the war, this building was also a hospital. After the war, it served as offices for the Columbia Post Office, the federal military commander of the Columbia District and the state treasurer. The legislature used the chapel for meetings.

G. The President's House

Built in 1854, it was not used during the war because it was another faculty residence. Though the student body had left the school to join the Confederate army, the faculty remained and continued to live in their on-campus residences.

H. LeGare College

On the top floor of this 1848 building is Clariosophic Hall, home of the Clariosophic Literary Society. The society's members included John C. Calhoun, Andrew Jackson, General Wade Hampton III and Robert Mills. Before the war, the society's chambers were said to be finer than the chambers of the State House.

At one time, General Winfield Scott, commander of the U.S. Army and the hero of the Mexican-American War, was part of its roster, and the group took great pride in his membership. However, when he sided with the North (Scott hailed from Virginia), he was expelled and replaced with thirteen men who served as Confederate generals, among them General P.G.T. Beauregard.

During the war, the commandant of Confederate troops and provost marshal for Columbia had their offices here. After the war, the South Carolina State Senate used Clariosophic Hall as its meeting place.

I. Pinckney College

This 1837 building was also used as a hospital.

J. Lieber College

Named for the professor expelled by the Euphradians, this circa 1837 faculty residence was where Lieber once lived.

There are three other prewar buildings located along the perimeter of the Horseshoe.

K. Flinn Hall

Located behind the World War Memorial

Built in 1858 as another faculty residence, this house originally stood on the corner of Pendleton and Sumter Streets. During the war years, this was the home of Professor Joseph LeConte, a noted geologist of his day and chairman of physics at South Carolina College. LeConte was also in charge of the Confederate chemical labs located on Elmwood Avenue (see #46).

Perhaps more importantly to scholars, Professor LeConte had a bright, articulate teenage daughter named Emma. Emma kept a diary during the war that was later published as *When the World Ended*, and her description of the sack and occupation of Columbia is one of the most vivid first-person accounts of that terrible tragedy. Her father's diary account of those troubled days was also published as *'Ware Sherman?*

The house barely survived the 1865 fire. In 1935, it was moved to its present location to make way for the memorial. After an electrical fire in 1995, the interior was gutted and the exterior was renovated to restore more of its nineteenth-century appearance.

L. Old Observatory

Located on Pendleton Street, behind DeSaussure College

Built in 1852, a seven-inch revolving brass telescope was mounted here. Both the building and the equipment were badly damaged during the burning of Columbia.

M. Longstreet Theater

Intersection of Sumter and Greene Streets

Originally built in the middle of Sumter Street, it was named for school president Augustus B. Longstreet, a noted secessionist and a cousin of Lee's "War Horse" Lieutenant General James Longstreet. Built as an auditorium originally named College Hall in 1855, it was plagued with bad luck from the start. The building was finished two years late and had its roof blown off twice. Upon its completion, it was quickly discovered that the acoustics were so poor that it was useless as an auditorium.

During the war years, the building was used as a hospital and morgue. In October 1865, the legislature reconvened here, with the Senate in the basement and the House upstairs. However, the bad acoustics forced the lawmakers to move to the Horseshoe. The auditorium was then used as a stable. From 1870 to 1887, it served as an armory and arsenal. From 1888 to 1893, it was a science facility before becoming a gymnasium until 1976, when its interiors were gutted and replaced by a theater in the round.

N. Thomas Cooper Library

1322 Greene Street

During Reconstruction, the Federal army used as a parade ground the area now occupied by the reflecting pool. Located in the Thomas Cooper Library's southern side is the Ernest F. Hollings Special Collections Library. The Irvin Department of Rare Books & Special Collections includes the Francis Lord Collection of over three thousand rare and valuable books about the Civil War, most of which are firsthand accounts from the Federal perspective.

Across the street from the library is the postwar Preston College. In 1865, this spot was a grassy field where many a homeless Columbian stayed while the city burned.

For information on the Irvin Department of Rare Books & Special Collections, call (803) 777-3847 or visit www.sc.edu/library/spcoll/rarebook.html.

For more information on visiting the University of South Carolina main campus, go to www.sc.edu/visitors.

27. HOWARD'S HEADQUARTERS (MCCORD-JONES HOUSE)

1431 Pendleton Street, northwest corner of Bull and Pendleton Streets

This Greek Revival house was built in 1849 by David James McCord (1797–1855), who was a lawyer, planter and intendant, or mayor, of Columbia. He was also a state legislator and president of the Bank of South Carolina. In addition, McCord was editor of the *Telescope*, a leading pro-nullification newspaper.

McCord-Jones House (Howard's headquarters), where Major General Oliver Otis Howard learned that Columbia was on fire.

His wife, Louisa McCord (1810–1879), was a successful author of political and economic essays, poetry and drama. During the Civil War, she served as the nursing director for the hospital at South Carolina College. People from all over Columbia brought her food to feed the patients of the hospital. Some patients came to her house to be fed.

General Howard set up his headquarters in this house. Howard (1860–1909) was an intelligent man, having taught mathematics at his alma mater, West Point. A very pious man who once considered giving up the military for the ministry, he tried to outlaw swearing in the ranks. Not surprisingly, this directive failed. Despite this, he was well liked by both officers and enlisted men.

Regarded as a brave officer, he lost an arm at the Battle of Seven Pines, for which he received the Congressional Medal of Honor. Howard was often criticized for his performance on the battlefield; however, as Sherman's second in command, he made few mistakes and carried out all of his superior's orders without a problem and earned the lifelong respect of Sherman.

While he was resting, Howard learned that the city was on fire. He left the house and headed into the streets to direct the efforts to restore order and control the flames.

The next day, officials from South Carolina College came to this house to ask Howard for protection. On February 19, when a group of civic leaders went to Sherman to request food, medicines and guns to keep order when the army left, Sherman referred them to Howard, saying, "Howard runs the religion of this army…He will treat you better than one of your own generals." Howard agreed to leave some supplies, but what he gave left much to be desired.

Howard gave five hundred head of cattle that were described as "extremely poor," "starving" and "dying of exhaustion at the rate of fifteen to twenty head per diem." One resident complained that Sherman "gave us nothing to feed [the cattle] and a hundred and sixty of them died of starvation before they could be killed." Still, it was better than nothing, and local officials were soon issuing rations of food to the civilian population. These cattle were kept in the brick walls of South Carolina College since there was no other place to pen them within the city.

As for the rest of the supplies, the medicine, besides a pint of castor oil, was only enough to fill a large cigar box. Howard also left behind one hundred old muskets that had to be repaired before they could be used.

After the war, Howard headed the Freedmen's Bureau, the federal agency in charge of assimilating freed slaves into society, and founded Howard University in Washington, D.C. Later he fought in the Western Indian Plains War and served as superintendent of the U.S. Military Academy. From 1886 until his retirement in 1894, he was commander of the army's Division of the East. Upon retiring, he settled in Vermont, where he devoted his last years to writing and educational efforts. He died in 1909.

Howard's legacy lived on in Columbia for years to come. In 1869, a school opened for freed slaves, named the Howard School in his honor. For decades it was the only school for African Americans in the city (see #49).

28. Horry-Guignard House

1527 Senate Street

General Peter Horry, the second in command to General Francis Marion, the legendary Swamp Fox of the American Revolution, built this house prior to 1813. This is one of the oldest buildings in Columbia and one of the few prewar residences still standing south of Gervais Street.

Local legend states that this home was saved by the culinary skills of a slave named Dilcie. Left to tend to the house after her master's family had

Horry-Guignard House. Legend states that the cooking skills of a slave saved this home from destruction.

fled, she allegedly went to Sherman's headquarters and offered "the best cooking in Columbia." Some officers decided to take advantage of the offer and went to the house to eat a chicken dinner she prepared. Dilcie's cooking skills must have been as good as she claimed, for the officers "gave" her this house and all its contents, which were left unmolested.

29. Sherman's Headquarters Site

Clarion Town House Hotel, 1500 block of Gervais Street

This two-story town house–style building sits on the site where Sherman had his headquarters in 1865. Then, a two-story framed house owned by Blanton Duncan of Kentucky sat here. Duncan had fled the city out of fear that he would be arrested since he was contracted to print Confederate money. Duncan's home featured a large wine cellar, which was mistaken by Federal troops for a slave dungeon.

During the day of February 17, Sherman visited with an old friend, Miss Poyas, a sister of James Poyas, an old hunting companion of Sherman when the general was stationed at Fort Moultrie. Unlike many of her neighbors, Miss Poyas's home and property were unmolested. Sherman noticed ducks and chickens in the yard and "a general air of peace and comfort that was really pleasant to behold at that time of universal desolation." Sherman and Miss Poyas had a pleasant visit; the general asked about her family and her brother James. Curiosity got the better of Sherman, who had to ask why her property was untouched. "I owe it to you, general," was her reply. "Not at all," responded Sherman. "I did not know you were here till a few minutes ago."

At that point, she handed the general a book. "You remember, when you were at our house on Cooper River in 1845, you gave me a book," which he had inscribed "to Miss — Poyas, with the compliments of W.T. Sherman, First-lieutenant Third artillery." Miss Poyas had gotten the book out when Hampton left the city. When some Federals had entered her house and yard and started to steal her poultry, she approached one of them and asked him in the name of his general to protect her property.

The man said to her, "What do you know of Uncle Billy?" To which she answered, "Why, when he was a young man he used to be our friend in Charleston, and here is a book he gave me." The soldier took the book, read the inscription and then turned to his companions, saying, "Boys, that's so; that's Uncle Billy's writing, for I have seen it often before." He ordered all pillaging to stop and had a guard placed at her home.

Sherman asked her how her guard had been, to which she responded by stating that he was a good man from Iowa who was in another room looking after her baby. He had chased away some would-be looters just five minutes before Sherman's arrival. Sherman stayed for "a long social visit" and saw to it that she received some rice and one hundred pounds of ham from his own mess.

Sherman also visited another Charleston acquaintance, Mrs. Harris Simons, sister-in-law of the Honorable James Simons, an old friend of the general.

Sherman later met Mayor Goodwyn at this site. "[Sherman] appeared very social, spoke kindly and friendly, and promised me most faithfully that our city should be protected and as safe as if it was in my own hands… he wished to be particular in not injuring any private property" and he promised that "we did not intend to stay long."

In a second meeting with the mayor, Sherman told Goodwyn that it was his "duty to destroy some of the public or government buildings: but I shall reserve this performance to another day. It shall be done to-morrow, provided the [winds] be calm." Again he reassured Mayor Goodwyn that "not a finger's breadth…of your city shall be harmed. You may lie down to sleep, satisfied that your town shall be as safe in my hands as if wholly in your own." An exhausted Sherman then went to bed.

About 11:00 p.m., Sherman learned that the city was on fire. According to his memoirs, he ran from the house to help direct efforts to put out the blaze. The morning after the fire, Sherman was so besieged by requests that he and his officers complained that they could not get any work done because the army was busy trying to answer all the requests for protection.

The house survived the fire and was later remodeled. After the war, Duncan offered to sell his home to the state as a governor's mansion, but the offer was declined due to a lack of funds in the state's treasury. Unfortunately, the house could not survive "progress" and was torn down in the 1960s to make room for this hotel.

30. Woods Headquarters/Last Home of Wade Hampton III

Southeast corner of Senate and Barnwell Streets, at the Hampton House Apartments

Fifteenth Corps' First Division commander Major General Charles Woods made his headquarters on this site.

Coincidentally, in 1899 the citizens of South Carolina would buy a house on this site for Confederate General Wade Hampton III when his home, Southern Cross, burned down. He lived here until his death in 1902. Hampton's home was later destroyed to make way for the apartment building currently on the site.

Robert Mills House Area

Hampton, Barnwell, Bull and Richland Streets bound this area. In 1865, this was one of the premier residential areas in Columbia.

31. Methodist Female College Site

Historic marker on Hampton Street between Pickens and Henderson Streets

The school was founded in 1854 by the South Carolina Conference of the Methodist Episcopal Church "to educate young women for fruitful service to church, state and nation." The first classes were held on this site in 1859, and the school remained in operation during the war.

During the occupation, some soldiers thought the school was a military academy and came close to burning it until the truth was told. Legend says that the school's music professor, W.H. Orchard, heard that all unoccupied buildings in Columbia would be burned by a certain hour. Upon learning this, he went to the school and stood in its doorway so that the Yankees could see him. In 1905, it relocated to its present campus on North Main Street.

32. Chesnut Cottage

1718 Hampton Street

This is an example of a "Columbia Cottage," the most common home style in the city in the 1860s, a one-and-a-half-story house on a raised basement. Camden natives Brigadier General James Chesnut (1815–1885) and his wife, Mary (1823–1886), rented this house from fall 1864 to early winter 1865. Much of Mrs. Chesnut's *A Diary from Dixie*, one of the most famous first-person accounts of the war, was written here.

On October 5, 1865, Confederate President Jefferson Davis visited his old friends the Chesnuts here en route to Richmond from inspecting Confederate troops in Georgia. Just before breakfast, Davis and his aides, Custis Lee (the son of General Lee) and former Texas Governor Francis Lubbock, arrived. After breakfast, General Chesnut and the aides went off together, leaving Mary and the president alone. Davis was relaxing on the porch when a couple of small boys came along. One of them stopped and yelled to the others, "Come here and look! There is a man on Mrs. Chesnut's porch who looks just like Jeff Davis on a postage stamp!" A crowd gathered, and Davis went inside.

Soon afterward, General Chesnut and his guests returned and told Davis that the crowd wanted to know if he would make an address about one o'clock. Davis readily agreed, and for good reason. In two months the state legislature would be having elections for governor, and it was expected that they were going to elect a governor who opposed his policies. Thus, Davis was in no position to refuse.

Chesnut Cottage. Brigadier General James Chesnut and his wife, Mary, leased this house. Here they entertained Confederate President Jefferson Davis. Mrs. Chesnut wrote much of her famous diary here.

Mary Chesnut.

At the requested hour, Davis stepped on the porch. The crowd had grown so large that Mary Chesnut and some of her friends had to go into the bedroom reserved for the president and open the window facing the porch to hear him speak. An honor guard of cadets from the Arsenal Academy greeted him, along with a brass band. The mayor of Columbia, Thomas Goodwyn, made some introductory remarks, and then Davis spoke.

Mary Chesnut's diary makes no mention of Davis writing a speech or plans for him to make any public appearances in Columbia. Given Davis's oratory skills, his remarks could have been impromptu. Then again, he had just made an appearance in Augusta and may have recycled his speech from there.

Davis started his speech by referring to the American Revolution and the role that South Carolina had played in that struggle and the similar odds it faced now. He commended the state for its courage and sacrifice while attacking those who called for returning to the Union. Davis also attacked the North for refusing peace negotiations. He appealed to those who could serve in the army to do so, saying, "Is it not the time for every man capable of bearing arms to say: My country needs my services, and my country shall have them!"

Davis also expressed confidence in General John Hood, despite the fact that he had given up Atlanta after four costly defeats. "Hood's strategy has been good and his conduct gallant. His eye is now fixed upon a point far beyond that where he was assailed by the enemy," said Davis, adding, "I see no chance for Sherman to escape from a defeat or a disgraceful rout."

Davis ended his remarks with an appeal for support of his policies: "I only ask you to have faith and confidence and to believe that every faculty of my head and my heart is devoted to your cause and to that I shall, if necessary, give my own life." He closed with a reference to Hood's plans, stating, "I believe it is the powers of the men of the Confederacy to plant our banners on the banks of the Ohio where we may say to the Yankee, 'be quiet, or we shall teach you another lesson.'"

Sherman obtained a copy of the speech and, after reading it, came to the conclusion that the fall of Atlanta had "broke upon Jeff. Davis so suddenly as to disturb the equilibrium of his usually well-balanced temper, so that… he let out some thoughts, which otherwise he would have kept to himself," adding that Davis seemed to "have lost all sense and reason." Sherman wryly commented that "to be forewarned was to be forearmed, and I think we took full advantage of the occasion."

After the speech, Davis was "thoroughly exhausted" and his hand was "nearly shaken off" by well-wishers. To help revive the president, Mrs. Chesnut had a mint julep ready for him. Mary also received an unexpected bonus. Friends and supporters of Davis came by and brought food, fine wines and even china for the president's dinner.

Davis would tell his wife that he had the best ham, coffee and Madeira wine in a long time in Columbia. This was not just a polite compliment. Thanks to runaway inflation, the larder of the Confederate White House had become rather meager, and due to the pressures of the war, Davis sometimes went all day without eating.

Though Davis was optimistic about Hood's chances, Custis Lee told Mary that things were bad for the Confederacy. Though he did not say so, she inferred that Lee had no confidence in Hood, writing, "This movement of the western army is against common sense." Mrs. Chesnut knew Hood very well, and though she did not share it, she agreed more with the younger Lee than with Davis.

After dinner, Davis and his party left Columbia for Richmond. Six months later, Davis would return to South Carolina, not as the president of a nation, but as a fugitive fleeing from the Federal army.

Mary "was so tired" from the visit but could not rest. "For a week I was busy gathering up stray dishes and serviettes." She did "not touch pen or paper" for ten days. She did receive a letter from Varina Davis, the wife of the president, thanking Mary for giving her husband a "delightful" visit with "the best hostess in the world."

When Sherman neared Columbia, General Chesnut sent Mary to North Carolina for safety, though he stayed in Columbia until the Confederates evacuated the city. During the evacuation, General Chesnut overslept and was only awakened by an explosion at a train depot. He quickly got up and discovered that almost every Confederate soldier was gone and that the mayor was surrendering the city. Luckily, he was able to safely join Hampton's cavalry at Killians and would join his wife.

The Chesnuts never returned to this house. After the war, Mary continued to work on her diary. Published posthumously, it became a bestseller that has never been out of print. Ironically, Mary hated the term "Dixie." An annotated version of the diary, containing previously unpublished material, came out in 1981 under the title *Mary Chesnut's Civil War* and won the Pulitzer Prize. Mrs. Chesnut was honored on a U.S. postage stamp in 1995.

Somehow this house survived both the fire and "progress." Once used as a doctor's office, the house today is a bed-and-breakfast inn.

Contact the Chesnut Cottage Bed and Breakfast Inn at (803) 256-1718 or visit www.chesnutcottage.com.

33. Columbia Theological Seminary (Robert Mills House)

1616 Blanding Street

Local merchant Ainsley Hall commissioned Robert Mills to design this house in 1823, after he sold his house across the street to General Wade Hampton I. Though Mills designed numerous public buildings around Columbia and across South Carolina, he seldom designed houses, so this structure is a rarity.

Sadly, Hall died before occupying his new home. His widow was forced to sell it to the Presbyterian Synod of South Carolina and Georgia for use as a

Columbia Theological Seminary (Robert Mills House). Many citizens flocked to the seminary's grounds for safety the night of the fire.

seminary in 1831. The mansion was used for offices and classrooms, while two large dormitories flanked the building. A carriage house on Henderson Street was used as a chapel.

Because of the spacious grounds around the building, and since it was across the street from the headquarters of Major General John Logan's headquarters, many Columbians fled here during the fire. However, a Federal soldier with a twisted sense of humor warned the refugees that when everyone was asleep they were going to burn the place, leading to a sleepless night for those inside.

The school reopened after the war. Its postwar faculty included Reverend Joseph R. Wilson, father of future U.S. President Woodrow Wilson. In the carriage house, Winthrop Training School, predecessor of modern-day Winthrop University, was founded in 1886.

In 1925, the seminary was relocated to Decatur, Georgia. Columbia Bible College used the site until the 1950s. In the 1960s, when the site was about to be turned into a parking lot, the property was purchased and restored by the newly formed Historic Columbia Foundation.

Today, only the original house remains. The dormitories were torn down in the 1960s, while the carriage house was moved to the campus of Winthrop University in Rock Hill in 1936. The interior of the house is decorated to reflect the style of the nineteenth century.

The Historic Columbia Foundation offers tours of the house. Admission is charged. Call (803) 252-1770 or visit www.historiccolumbia.org for more information.

34. Hampton-Preston House

1600 Blanding Street

Ainsley Hall also built this house in 1818. According to tradition, Robert Mills was the architect. In 1823, Hall sold this house to General Wade Hampton, a hero of the American Revolution and the War of 1812. Hall was not interested in selling it, but Hampton was one of the wealthiest men in America and could meet any price Hall set.

After Hampton's death in 1835, his daughter Caroline and her husband, John S. Preston, moved in. For thirteen years, they traveled between family properties in the United States and Europe before settling down in this home in 1848. After that, it became a center of social life in Columbia. Its gardens, accented with sculptures from Europe, were world renowned for their beauty and grace.

Hampton-Preston House. Major General John Logan used this house as his headquarters. It was spared destruction thanks to the intervention of a feisty nun.

Preston was active in state and regional politics and was a friend of Jefferson Davis. Davis appointed him superintendent of the Bureau of Conscript in 1863 with the rank of lieutenant colonel. He was promoted to brigadier general in 1864.

On February 5, 1865, General John Bell Hood arrived in Columbia en route to Richmond. He had just resigned as commander of the Confederate Army of Tennessee because of his defeat at the Battle of Nashville in December 1864. Hood stayed with the Prestons for three days. Hood was strongly attracted to their daughter, Sally "Buck" Preston, who was considered one of the most beautiful women in the Confederacy. Some historians believe that Hood's decisions in the Atlanta and Nashville Campaigns of 1864 were a result of his desire to impress her so much that she would marry him.

Though Hood gave his friends a "heart-full greeting," he was obviously very depressed. John Preston Jr. observed that Hood had "absent fits" that were impossible to prevent and trying on the nerves of those around the general. "He looks in the fire and forgets me and seems going through in his own mind the torture of the damned," young Preston told Mary Chesnut.

From here General Butler's cavalry retreated from Columbia on the morning of February 17. Joining Butler's eight-hundred-man cavalry were the Arsenal cadets, who had manned a small battery along the Congaree River. The Confederates lined up from present-day Elmwood down to South Carolina College. Colonel U.R. Brooks recalled, "Words fail me to express how these battle-scared veterans looked. They were ready to spill every drop of their life's blood in defense of the helpless women and children. Some said it was time to fight, let us charge; while others said how glorious to die defending our beautiful city."

One cavalryman remembered, "In this position we remained until the head of Sherman's column reached some distance down Main Street, only a few blocks off. Hampton seemed loath to leave the city, and it was said he had occupied the position with the intention of charging the enemy, but Gen. Beauregard…would not allow it."

Beauregard opposed fighting in the streets because of the disproportionate number of women and children in Columbia. Because of the massive and chaotic exodus, the population of twenty thousand was down to an estimated twelve to fifteen thousand, with "the larger proportion being females and children and Negroes" and the white male population being "chiefly old men." Modern estimates put the ratio of women to men at forty to one.

Butler positioned himself on a small hill at the intersection of Main and Laurel Streets, which gave him a bird's-eye view of the arrival of the Federals. He observed Sherman's army for about an hour, watching them march through Cotton Town and then down Main Street until Sherman's advance was within a few hundred yards of him. Butler then retreated to the Preston mansion, where he watched the United States flag move down Main Street to the State House. About 10:30 a.m. he ordered, "Right about, march!" and the tiny Confederate army went on its way. Butler claimed that Columbia "was free from incendiarism" when he left.

As the soldiers left, frightened women cried out, "What! Leave us… leave us in the hands of the dreaded foe? Then God have mercy upon us poor helpless deserted women." To which one officer replied, "The city's surrendered. The army has gone."

When Sherman's troops occupied the city, Fifteenth Corps commander Major General John "Black Jack" Logan (1826–1886) used this house as his headquarters. At the start of the war, Logan was a Democratic congressman from Illinois who opposed the election of Abraham Lincoln, believing it would lead to war. However, after he witnessed the Union rout at the Battle of First Manassas, he was so disgusted that he grabbed a rifle and started firing at the Confederates.

Logan went back to Illinois and raised a regiment. Despite a lack of formal military training or experience, he rose through the ranks to become commander of the Fifteenth Corps with the rank of major general. He is generally regarded as one of the best Union corps commanders and the best Northern civilian general of the war.

Logan was the true victor at the Battle of Atlanta, taking temporary command of the Army of the Tennessee when its commander was killed early in the battle. Rallying the men on the field, Logan turned a near Confederate victory into a major Union victory. For this Logan expected to be given permanent command of the army, but he was passed over in favor of Howard because Logan was not a West Point graduate. To Logan's credit, he held no ill will toward Howard, and the two men worked well together, but Logan would hold a lifelong grudge against "the West Point clique."

Tradition says that Logan chose this house as "payback" to General Preston's brother, William C. Preston. The former U.S. congressman and senator had been a political rival and once called Logan an "Indian half-breed." Logan was on the verge of burning the house until the sisters of the Ursaline Convent stepped in and intervened (see #50).

Logan became one of the nation's most powerful politicians after the war, serving in both the U.S. House and Senate. In 1884, he was the unsuccessful Republican nominee for vice president of the United States. In Washington, he got back at "the West Point clique" by successfully introducing legislation that reduced the size of the army and significantly cut the pay of army officers, including Sherman, though Logan made peace with his former commander prior to his death.

Logan was also deeply involved in veteran activities. He founded the Society of the Army of the Tennessee and the Grand Army of the Republic. He is often credited with the idea of setting aside a day to honor those who died in war, called Decoration Day, the forerunner of today's Memorial Day.

The house was returned to the Prestons after the war, but financial problems forced the family to sell it in 1873 to Governor F.J. Moss, who used it for his residence. Later, the Ursuline Convent reoccupied it from 1887 to 1890. In 1890, it became the College for Women of the Presbyterian Church. In 1915, Chicora College for Women moved from Greenville, South Carolina, to the house and occupied it until 1930.

Afterward, the house was used as a boarding home. The lot was subdivided, and a car dealership replaced the fine, formal gardens. In the late 1960s, the State of South Carolina acquired the block for the state's 1970 tricentennial celebration. The home was restored at that time, and when the tricentennial ended, it was given to the Historic Columbia Foundation.

Today the house is restored to its prewar appearance and furnished with many pieces belonging to the Hampton and Preston families. An ongoing project has been the restoration of the once elaborate gardens.

The Historic Columbia Foundation offers tours of the house. Admission is charged. Call (803) 252-1770 or visit www.historiccolumbia.org for more information.

35. Howe House

1531 Blanding Street, on the northwest corner of Blanding and Pickens Streets

This unusually shaped house, built circa 1850, was the home of Dr. George Howe, a professor at the Presbyterian Seminary. Dr. Howe's wife, Anna, was the sister of Martha Roosevelt, the mother of future U.S. President Theodore Roosevelt. The house survived destruction due to the family's Northern ties.

During his administration (1901–1909), President Roosevelt ordered the War Department to return all captured Confederate battle flags to the state from which they originated. This act healed some of the lingering wounds from the war. Roosevelt also offered former General Wade Hampton III the easy and lucrative position of postmaster of Columbia if he would switch to the Republican Party. Though he desperately needed the money, Hampton declined, saying his name could not be bought.

Dr. Howe's son, George Jr., married Annie Josephine Wilson, sister of President Woodrow Wilson, the first post–Civil War southern-born president. Ironically, Wilson defeated Roosevelt in the 1912 presidential election.

36. Site of Christ Episcopal Church (Good Shepherd Episcopal Church)

1512 Blanding Street

One of the most beautiful Episcopal churches in South Carolina was built on this site in 1860. The large edifice stretched half the length of the block on both sides. Several accounts suggest that the church was one of the last buildings set on fire that terrible night.

Site of Christ Episcopal Church (Good Shepherd Episcopal Church). One of Barnard's most famous photographs shows the remains of one of Columbia's largest churches, which was said to be one of the last buildings torched.

A picture of its ruins is one of the most famous and graphic photographs of Sherman's devastation. Emma LeConte described it as a "beautiful ruin." Columbians often visited the ruins on moonlit nights because allegedly one could see "strange apparitions" that many believed were angels because they hovered over the site of the altar.

Though the walls remained for some time, the church was never rebuilt. Today, only the cornerstone of the old church remains under the steps of the modern church. The 1900 laying of Good Shepherd's cornerstone was presided over by Bishop Ellison Capers (1837–1908), a brigadier general in the Confederate army.

For more on the current church's history, visit www.goodshepherdcolumbia.org.

37. CRAWFORD-CLARKSON HOUSE

1502 Blanding Street, on the southeast corner of Blanding and Bull Streets

This unusual nineteenth-century home features two glass columns with shelves that flank the entrance to the 1838 Federal-style town house. They were used to display rare and exotic plants that the house's original owner, John Crawford, a prominent Irish-born banker, collected. His descendants still own the building.

Two legends explain how the house was saved. One is that John's unmarried sister, Margaret, begged a Federal officer to save the house. Moved by her courage, the officer provided a guard. The other legend states that a loyal

Crawford-Clarkson House. One of Columbia's most unusual nineteenth-century homes is still owned by descendants of the house's original owner.

slave met some soldiers at the door and begged them to save the house as it had just been given to her.

Several colorful tales surround this house during the Federal occupation. One involves Crawford's attempt to save his favorite horse, a white stallion. Crawford took the animal inside and led up him up the steps to the second floor, apparently oblivious to the dangers of leaving it in a wooden house surrounded by burning buildings. Crawford also managed to safely bury his and the First Presbyterian Church's silver.

Though the house was spared, it was ransacked. Federal troops put a bayonet through a secretary desk to make sure that no Confederates were hiding in it. Despite the presence of a guard, the family watched the city burn in the cemetery of First Presbyterian Church. All they brought with them was a copper teakettle, in which they made tea to keep them warm during the cold night.

Sherman's visit had a lasting impression on one slave named Mauma, a nursemaid to the Crawfords. She remained with the family after the war. Three decades later, when soldiers about to go fight in the Spanish-American War came visiting wearing their blue uniforms, Mauma chased them down the steps with a broom shouting, "Yankees! Yankees!"

38. Maxcy Gregg House

1518 Richland Street, between Bull and Pickens Streets

Maxcy Gregg built this Classic Revival house in 1840. Douglas Southall Freeman in *Lee's Lieutenants* describes Gregg as "culturally one of the best-furnished men of the Confederacy. Few knew Greek dramatists or the philosophers so thoroughly. Perhaps none combined so precise a knowledge of botany, of ornithology, of astronomy. A scholar he was, a scientist and a gentleman."

Gregg was a successful lawyer who served as a major in the Mexican-American War. An active promoter of states' rights, Gregg helped draft and later signed the Ordinance of Secession. In January 1861, Gregg formed the First South Carolina Regiment of troops and served as its colonel. The troops were signed for six months and sent to Charleston to participate in the siege of that city. Later, those who stayed past their initial six months saw action at First Manassas. In December, Gregg was promoted to brigadier general and commanded a brigade of three regiments.

Gregg was famous for his courage. His brigade lost more men in the Seven Days' Campaign than any other brigade in A.P. Hill's division. Offsetting Gregg's fine attributes as a commander was a notorious temper that led him to personally clash with his corps commander, Lieutenant General Thomas "Stonewall" Jackson, on policy and strategy. When Jackson ordered the arrest of two of Gregg's colonels, the South Carolinian filed charges against Jackson, though at the request of General Robert E. Lee the charges were dropped.

Maxcy Gregg House. Despite being ransacked by Union soldiers, the house survived the fire and is now used as offices.

A rifle ball at the Battle of Fredericksburg mortally wounded Gregg in December 1862. He lay in agony for two days, fully awake as doctors and friends looked on, helpless to ease his suffering. Jackson made a personal visit to his dying lieutenant and the two men made peace, a scene dramatized in the film *Gods and Generals*.

Despite his pain, Gregg dictated a farewell to the governor of South Carolina, saying, "If I am to die now, I give my life cheerfully for the independence of South Carolina." Mercifully, he died on December 15, 1862. Robert E. Lee eulogized Gregg, calling him a "brave soldier and accomplished gentleman." Likewise, Jackson called Gregg "a brave and accomplished officer, full of heroic sentiment and chivalrous honor. He had rendered valuable service in this great struggle for our freedom, and the country has much reason to deplore the loss sustained by his premature death."

Gregg's body was returned to Columbia by a leased slave named William Rose, née William Barrett, to whom Gregg left his general's coat, a sword and his gold pocket watch. Rose proudly wore them in a photo taken at a reunion of Confederate veterans. The watch is now on display at the South Carolina Confederate Relic Room and Military Museum. Rose is also credited with arranging the deathbed meeting between Gregg and Jackson.

Born in 1813, Rose led an interesting life. He had accompanied previous masters in the Seminole War and the Mexican War. In the latter, he brought home the body of Colonel Pierce M. Butler.

Rose was an active campaign worker for Wade Hampton III in the 1876 gubernatorial election. Afterward, he worked as a porter to several South Carolina governors in the State House and was an elder of Ladsen Presbyterian Church. Rose remained associated with the state militia for the rest of his life. At a full-dress inspection of the South Carolina State Militia prior to their deployment to Cuba to fight in the Spanish-American War, he was a guest of honor.

Rose was the subject of a flattering article in the *New York Times* in August 1897 that described him as the most popular black man in the state. He died about 1901 and was buried in a state militia uniform befitting his honorary rank of captain.

During the occupation of Columbia, Gregg's home was sacked and several personal possessions were stolen. His secretary desk was smashed to pieces, but the home somehow escaped serious damage.

After the war, Columbians honored the general by naming a street and a park after him. A large monument marks his grave at Elmwood Cemetery. A lifelong bachelor, he is buried with his parents.

39. State Hospital (the Asylum)

2100 Bull Street, at the intersection of Bull Street and Elmwood Avenue

The horseshoe-shaped Greek Revival building on the right of the main entrance is the original building designed by Robert Mills circa 1827. The revolutionary design featured large corridors, windows in patients' rooms facing the building's sunnier southern side and a unique central heating system. Like most of Mills's buildings, it is fireproof.

From December 1864 until February 1865, the Asylum was the home for Federal prisoners of war who had been kept at Camp Sorghum (see #7). The new camp was nicknamed "Camp Asylum," though some called it "Camp Lunacy." Days prior to Federal occupation, most prisoners were transported by rail to Charlotte.

During the night of the fire, many families went to the spacious lawn of the complex to avoid the flames. Afterward, the Seventeenth Corps, which Sherman called into Columbia to help maintain order after the fire, also used the grounds for its camp. The corps' commander, Major General Francis Blair, made his headquarters in a house near this site.

According to David Conyngham, a reporter from the *New York Herald*, a number of survivors of the fire were admitted as patients to the hospital; the shock of the events of the night of February 17 had caused them to lose their minds. Conyngham also saw many desperate people roaming aimlessly through the streets of the city.

40. Hale-Elmore-Seibels House

1601 Richland Street on the northeast corner of Pickens and Richland Streets

Built about 1796, this house is considered the oldest structure in the city of Columbia. In the back is a separate brick building originally used as a kitchen. From 1860 until 1984, it was in the Seibels family. Since 1984, the Historic Columbia Foundation has owned it and rents it out for meetings and receptions.

During the Federal occupation of Columbia, a faithful slave buried a pot of gold in the gardens when Sherman's army neared the city. When the troops entered the city, they tried to get the slave to tell them where he had hidden it by hanging the man from a tree until he was close to suffocation and then letting him down. They repeated this several times. Eventually, the slave died without revealing the location. Sadly, this was not an uncommon event. Many slaves across South Carolina were tortured or killed by Union soldiers trying to learn the location of their masters' valuables.

The gold was never found but on moonlit nights, it is said that the ghost of an old, white-haired black man carrying a shovel can be seen in the gardens.

Note the median in the street in front of the house. It is the last remaining example of street medians, which were once common in the original part of the city.

The first floor and gardens of the Seibels House can be rented out for special events. Call (803) 252-7742, extension 11, or visit www.historiccolumbia.org for more information.

41. Friday Cottage

1830 Henderson Street

About 1840, Samuel David Friday built this small cottage. Friday served as a captain in the Confederate army and died during the war. His widow and two daughters turned the home into a boardinghouse. Legend states that the Fridays took in a sick Federal officer who had escaped from the prisoner of war camp at the State Hospital and that, in gratitude, he saw to it that the house was protected during Sherman's stay.

The Friday Cottage's ground floor is home to Palmetto & Luna Art Gallery and is open by appointment only. Call (803) 397-7686 or visit www.palmettoluna.org for more information.

Marion Street Area

This was also an upscale residential area in 1860 Columbia.

42. Site of the Blanding House

Northwest corner of Marion and Blanding Streets

On this site was the home of Abram Blanding (1776–1839). A native of Massachusetts, he was active in nineteenth-century civic matters, including the city's first waterworks. He helped build the Columbia Canal and was a cofounder of the Presbyterian Seminary. His house, said to be one of the finest in the city, was destroyed in the fire of February 17.

A slave loyal to the 1865 owners of the house buried some treasure in the yard. Yankee troops tried to torture the slave into telling where the valuables were buried, but he died before revealing their locations. Because his spirit was said to be seen at night protecting the valuables, owners of this property have had to chase off would-be treasure hunters.

43. De Burhl-Marshall Mansion

1401 Laurel Street, on the northeast corner of Laurel and Marion Streets

Built about 1820, this impressive mansion is one of the few brick antebellum homes still standing in Columbia. It may have been designed by Robert

Mills or based on his work. Confederate General Joseph Johnston moved into this home in the fall of 1864 and stayed until February 1865.

The attic timbers still bear the char marks that are said to have originated from an attempt by Union soldiers to start a fire in the attic. Luckily, Mrs. Marshall was able to talk the soldiers out of burning her home.

44. Mann-Simmons Cottage

1403 Richland Street on the northeast corner of Richland and Marion Streets

This Classic Revival house was probably built between 1825 and 1830 and owned by Celia Mann (1799–1867). A remarkable woman, Mann was a Charleston slave who bought her freedom and then walked all the way to Columbia to claim her home. How she acquired her freedom is unknown, but she had this property as early as 1844. The census of 1850 shows that Mann not only owned this house but also owned a seventy-one-year-old female slave who, according to tradition, was her mother.

Mann-Simmons Cottage. A freed slave who was a successful midwife owned this house.

Mann's situation was unusual but not unique. In 1850, 6 percent of all blacks in Columbia were free. Mann was active in the black community, organizing two churches in the basement of her home. She was also a popular and successful midwife. At the time of her death, her estate was valued at $1,500, and her obituary described her as having been "present at the birth of many of our citizens."

Family legend states that during the fire, Mann hid several families in her tiny basement because they felt that her house would be safe because Mrs. Mann was black. Legend also states that she hid the silver and valuables of many families in her house and yard.

Mann had four daughters. Three of them moved to the North, while the youngest, Agnes Jackson, stayed in Columbia and married musician Bill Simmons. Mrs. Mann left this house to Agnes, who lived there until her death in 1907. Through the Simmons branch of the family, descendants of Celia Mann still live in the city. For over one hundred years, this residence remained in Mann's family until 1970, when it was sold to the Columbia Housing Authority. Thanks to a grass-roots movement, the Historic Columbia Foundation took over site in the late 1970s and opened it as a museum in 1978.

Today, the interior of the house is restored to show how the family lived in the late nineteenth century. A 1998 archaeological study of the ground surrounding the house revealed eight thousand objects. Plans are now underway to restore the landscaping around the residence to a nineteenth-century appearance.

The Historic Columbia Foundation offers tours of the house. Admission is charged. Call (803) 252-1770 or visit www.historiccolumbia.org for more information.

Arsenal Hill Area

This area, except for site #50, is bounded by Elmwood Avenue, Assembly, Huger and Hampton Streets.

45. Elmwood Cemetery

501 Elmwood Avenue, on the west end of Elmwood Avenue, near I-126 and the Columbia Canal

Established in 1854 with 250 acres, the first body was interred here in 1856. Today Elmwood has over twenty-two thousand people buried over 91 acres. Among them are Confederate Generals Maxcy Gregg and Milledge L. Bonham. The cemetery also contains the Monument to the Unknown Confederate Dead, two Confederate cemeteries and the monument to the Confederate Soldier's Home.

Near one of the Confederate cemeteries is a speaker's stand and memorial arch. They were erected in 1951 by the United Daughters of the Confederacy. Each May, the state UDC, in conjunction with the South Carolina Division of the Sons of Confederate Veterans, has its annual Confederate Memorial Day Observance. Twenty-five of the graves in this cemetery are marked "unknown." The other cemetery contains members of the Wade Hampton Camp of the United Confederate Veterans.

Before Sherman's arrival in Columbia, a small artillery battery manned by Arsenal cadets was placed on the site along the banks of the canal, but

The Confederate cemetery at Elmwood Cemetery.

they saw no action. One of their cannons, which was buried on the property to prevent its capture, can be seen at the State Museum.

Elmwood Cemetery is open daily during daylight hours. Information is available at the entrance to the locations of the graves. Call (803) 252-2133 for more information.

46. COLUMBIA CANAL

Historic marker located on Gervais Street at the bridge in front of the State Museum (see #60). Access to the canal via Columbia Riverfront Park can be found at the west end of Laurel Street where it intersects with Huger Street.

In 1815, the state began construction of a twenty-two-mile system of canals, sluices and locks along the Saluda, Broad and Congaree Rivers, with Irish immigrants doing much of the labor. By 1824, the Columbia Canal was finished. However, the Columbia to Charleston water route was slow and not cost efficient. When the railroads came along in the 1840s, the canal fell into disuse.

Columbia Canal. This view from the canal's northern end shows approximately where Colonel George Stone crossed the waterway to get to Columbia.

The Confederate government leased the canal and built a powder works above the Gervais Street Bridge. These works survived the fire but were destroyed by Sherman. After the war, the Columbia Cotton Mill dammed up the canal at the Gervais Street Bridge to generate electricity. In the 1980s, the area was developed as a park.

Near the Huger Street entrance to the park is a historic marker commemorating the Howard School, the first public school for blacks in Columbia. This Reconstruction-era school was named after Sherman's second in command, General Oliver Otis Howard.

Riverfront Park is open daily during daylight hours. Call (803) 733-8331 or visit sites.google.com/site/columbiasriverfrontpark/home for more information.

47. SITE OF CONFEDERATE CHEMICAL PLANT

815 Elmwood Avenue on the modern-day Logan School site, just before I-126 on Elmwood Avenue

The South Carolina State Fair was held on this site from 1856 until 1861, when the grounds and buildings were converted into an army mobilization camp.

When the training camp was relocated to northeast Richland County, Professor Joseph LeConte of South Carolina College established the Confederate Mining and Nitrate Bureau on the site. LeConte also ran a chemical laboratory to produce medicines for the Confederate army and a government distillery that produced 250 gallons of "medicinal" whiskey and alcohol daily.

The buildings were also used for a hospital. When Sherman neared, LeConte tried to get his lab equipment out of the city. He succeeded, but the equipment was lost or destroyed outside of the city. Ironically, had he left it on the campus, it probably would have been spared.

Sherman's men burned the buildings on the site. Not until 1869 was the State Fair again held here. The last fair was held here in 1903. Ten years later, the Logan School was built on the site.

48. GOVERNOR'S MANSION COMPLEX

800 Richland Street between Laurel, Lincoln and Gadsden Streets

The Governor's Mansion complex consists of three historic houses that escaped the fire of February 17, 1865.

A. Officers' Quarters of the Arsenal Military Academy (the Governor's Mansion)

The Arsenal Military Academy was established here in 1842 by the state legislature as a preparatory school to train officers for the state militia. Students attended classes here for one to two years and then transferred to the Citadel in Charleston. Two multipurpose rectangular buildings were built on the site, situated on the highest point in the original city, which in time became known as Arsenal Hill, a name that is still used today.

In 1843, the school welcomed its first eight students. Nine years later, a large, three-story brick building that stretched along most of the Laurel

Arsenal Academy (South Carolina Governor's Mansion). The officers' barracks are all that remain of the state-run military prep school.

Street side of the block was built. In 1856, what is now the Governor's Mansion was built to house the faculty of the school. It would serve as officers' quarters throughout the rest of the school's brief history.

In 1861, the Citadel and the Arsenal were merged into the South Carolina Military Academy, and the cadets became the Battalion of State Cadets. At first, they were used to guard buildings and forts, but by 1864, the cadets were engaged in actual combat along the South Carolina coast. Later they were assigned to artillery batteries along the banks of the Congaree and Broad Rivers and guard duty at Camp Sorghum. They also did some minor skirmishing with Sherman's troops. When Governor Andrew Magrath evacuated the city, they served as an armed escort for him.

On May 1, 1865, the cadets, who were en route from Greenville to Newberry to be disbanded, fought a band of Union cavalrymen near Williamston in Anderson County in one of the last engagements of the war.

The school survived the burning of the city the night of February 17, but the dormitories, which could have been used to house the city's homeless, were destroyed the next day when Sherman's men razed the public buildings that had survived the disaster. Why the officers' quarters were spared is unclear.

On May 9, 1865, Governor Andrew Gordon Magrath disbanded the Arsenal cadets. With this action, the short history of the Arsenal Academy came to a close.

In 1868, Governor James L. Orr first proposed using the old officers' quarters as a governor's mansion. The legislature approved his recommendation and appropriated funds in 1868 and 1869 to do repairs and maintenance on the building and grounds. In 1869, the mansion was first used as the governor's residence, and it has been used almost continuously in that role since 1880.

B. The Caldwell-Hampton-Boylston House

This house was built about 1830 by John Caldwell, a successful local merchant. After the war, it was sold to Lucy and Caroline Hampton, nieces of Wade Hampton III.

The most famous occupant, however, was Mrs. Sarah Porter Smith Boylston, who bought the home in 1894 and lived here for sixty-nine years. Mrs. Boylston expanded her landholdings until she owned most of the land on the block. She turned it into a five-level garden that is still one of the finest in Columbia. She donated part of her garden to the Garden Club of South Carolina. In 1944, the garden became the first landscape memorial for veterans of World War II. Noted New York landscaper Loutrel Winslow Briggs donated his services for the garden's design in 1946. The State of South Carolina acquired the house in 1978.

C. The Lace House (Robertson House)

John Caldwell built this Classic Revival house about 1855 as a gift to his daughter Mary when she married Thomas J. Robertson of Fairfield County, who would represent South Carolina in the U.S. Senate during Reconstruction. Tradition says a New Orleans–based French architect designed the house. Because of the lacy ironwork on the porch and balcony, which was rare in this area, it became known as the "Lace House."

For thirteen years, this home was the headquarters for the South Carolina Women's Christian Temperance Union. In 1965, the Richland County Historic Preservation Commission bought the property and sold it to the state in 1967. It is now the official guesthouse of the state.

For information on tours of the Governor's Mansion call (803) 737-1710 or visit www.scgovernorsmansion.org.

49. Palmetto Armory/Palmetto Iron Works

Southeast corner of Laurel and Lincoln Streets, across from the Governor's Mansion

This white brick building, originally a sixty-four-foot, three-story-tall building, was built circa 1850 by Benjamin Flagg, an arms manufacturer, and James Boatwright. Shortly after its construction, they went into partnership with William Glaze, a renowned Columbia jeweler, silversmith and gunsmith. With Glaze as the senior partner, they turned it into the Palmetto Armory.

In 1851, they received a large state contract for weapons. When no other state contracts materialized, the armory became the Palmetto Iron Works. Glaze began making iron and brass farm and mill machines such as boilers and steam engines. In 1860, the works produced five hundred tons of goods.

When South Carolina left the Union, Glaze offered his facilities to the state. In February 1861, he began casting shells and later produced guns, bayonets, cartridges, sabers and rifle balls for South Carolina regiments. Glaze also produced cannons, and continued to make farm goods, during the war years. Although Glaze's building escaped destruction during the fire, Sherman ordered it destroyed on February 18.

After the war, Glaze had the building partially rebuilt and acquired new equipment. He took on George Shields, his foreman, as a partner. Shields became the senior partner, and consequently, the building was sometimes refereed to as "Shields' Foundry," though Palmetto Iron Works was still the official name. Sadly, Glaze could not revive his business, and by 1868, he

Palmetto Armory/ Palmetto Iron Works. Items that were made here are considered prized collector items.

filed for bankruptcy. Shields became the sole partner and continued to run the ironworks, while Glaze returned to jewelry making.

The building remained a foundry until it closed in 1927, and it stood empty until the City of Columbia bought it in 1941. The foundry section and smokestack were torn down, and the machine shop was adapted as a community center for which it is still used today.

Collectors of Civil War memorabilia consider the weapons that the armory put out among the most desired and valuable. Examples of these, as well as Glaze's silver work, are on display at the State Museum and the South Carolina Confederate Relic Room and Military Museum (#60).

50. SIDNEY PARK (FINLAY PARK)

930 Laurel Street, in the ravine between Assembly, Taylor, Laurel and Gadsden Streets

In 1820, Abram Blanding started construction of the city's first water plant. Two natural springs were tapped to feed the water lines. In 1826, at the cost of $75,000, almost all of it financed by Blanding, the plant was finished. Blanding had hoped to recoup his costs by selling the water to the public, but while the plant was hailed as a model of modern engineering, it was not profitable. In 1835, Blanding sold it to the city for $24,000. In 1855, the water plant was relocated to its present spot along the Columbia Canal.

Meanwhile, Algernon Sidney Johnston, a local newspaper editor, politician and the brother of future Confederate general Joseph Johnston, started promoting the idea of turning the site into a park. In 1850, the city appropriated funds for the park and incorporated several of Johnston's ideas. A painting of the park made before the war shows several water fountains and many green areas. A year later, the park opened to the public and quickly became one of the most popular places in the city to hear concerts and political meetings.

Sadly, Johnston did not enjoy his vision very long. He died in 1852. A year later, the city voted to name the park after him though for some unknown reason decided to use his middle name rather than his surname. Adding to the confusion, sometimes the park name is spelled "Sydney," though Johnston spelled his middle name with an "i" and not a "y."

During the fire, frightened citizens fled to the park to escape the flames, thinking that the wide, six-block area would be safe. Many of them were destitute, having just seen their homes and most of their belongings go up in flames. Eyewitness accounts suggest a scene similar to modern refugee camps. After Sherman left, people grazed animals in the park until the practice was banned the following May.

The park remained in existence until 1899, when the Seaboard Air Line Railroad talked the city into selling the property for a passenger station and freight depot that was relocated four years later. From then until the 1960s, the area was an industrial area, though talk occasionally surfaced about restoring the park. In 1960, the railroad gave the property back to the city to build a new post office on the Assembly Street side. This led to renewed interest in restoring the area to a park. Those plans came to fruition in 1990, when Sidney Park was rededicated. Later, it was renamed Finlay Park after the late Mayor Kirkman Finlay, who was instrumental in the return of the park.

Though the eighteen-acre park today bears little resemblance to its nineteenth-century predecessor, then as now, it is one of the most popular places in Columbia and is once again the scene of many a concert and public event.

The park is open daily. Call (803) 545-3100 for more information.

51. Site of the Ursuline Convent

1644 Main Street at the southeast corner of Blanding and Main Streets, the site of the old Tapp's Department Store

The Ursuline Convent was located on this site in a former seventy-room hotel that could house two hundred students. Tuition was $220 per month, which included room and board, washing, lights, fuel and English instruction. For an extra fee, instruction in foreign languages, singing, piano, harp, guitar, art and embroidery was offered. The school remained open throughout the war.

As Sherman neared Columbia, many non-Catholic girls were sent there for safety, as it was common knowledge that Sherman's wife, Ellen, and her family were devout Catholics; therefore, Sherman tried to spare Catholic churches and their properties to prevent the ire of his family. Even after Sherman occupied Columbia, girls were still being sent there.

While waiting to cross the Broad River, Sherman received a note from the mother superior of the Ursuline Convent, Sister Baptista Lynch. The sister had taught Sherman's daughter, Minnie, in an Ohio convent and therefore asked for protection for her school and pupils.

Sherman sent his inspector general, Colonel Charles Ewing, Ellen's brother, to personally deliver a message back to the mother superior informing her that both he and his army "contemplated no destruction of any private property in Columbia at all." However, a Catholic major from Detroit warned her "that she would need all the guard he had brought, as Columbia is a doomed city!" He had brought eight to ten guards, none of them Catholic, to the nun's dismay.

The warning was prophetic. When the fire broke out, the school's guards engaged in looting and pillaging. Soon the school itself was on fire. About 9:00 p.m., Sister Baptista had the girls gather up warm clothing and whatever possessions they could carry and assemble in a large classroom.

They went to the school's chapel, where Father Jeremiah Joseph O'Connell performed a benediction while the nuns and their charges recited the rosary. About 11:00 p.m., while performing the rituals, drunken soldiers burst through the doors of the chapel and rushed to steal the golden objects from the altar.

The girls were gathered in the main hall and then led three blocks to St. Peter's Catholic Church on Assembly Street. Reverend O'Connell led the group, defiantly holding a crucifix above his head, followed by the nuns and then the students. Remarkably, they made it to the church without serious incident, though the priest's watch was stolen. However, contrary to Sherman's promise, the convent was burned. Though convent officials had hidden several items on their person before the Union soldiers broke in, the school lost paintings, a harp and seventeen pianos.

At St. Peter's, two Irish Catholic Union officers were guarding the church, trying to protect it from the Union soldiers who had followed the nuns and their charges and were now trying to burn down the church. For safety, the girls were taken to the church cemetery, where they spent a cold and terrifying night. Thanks to the officers and an additional guard, the church survived the fire. Though the nuns and their charges were encouraged to come back inside the church, they chose to spend the night in the cemetery instead, all the while listening to taunts from the soldiers crying out, "We're just as holy as you are!…Now what do you think of God? Ain't Sherman greater?"

The next morning, Sherman went to the church and quickly learned that he had one very angry nun on his hands who personally accused him of deliberately breaking his promise to her. To get her off his back, and probably to avoid to the wrath of Mrs. Sherman as well, Sherman told Sister Baptista that she could choose any house in town she wanted.

The mother superior was quick in choosing. When she learned that the Preston Mansion (see #34), General Logan's headquarters, was to be destroyed, she chose it. Though the Prestons were not Catholics, they had befriended the nuns and supported the school.

Logan was on the verge of setting the house on fire. He had bales of straw all around the house when the nun informed him that Sherman said she could have this house. Logan did not believe her until she showed him the orders and even the title that Sherman had issued for it. A rather angry Logan ordered the combustibles removed.

Sherman had blankets and rations sent to the nuns and their charges, but the ordeal took its toll on two of the sisters, who were in "delicate" health and died.

After the war, the house and the ownership papers were given back to the Prestons. The Ursuline Convent reopened and, ironically, at one time operated out of the Preston Mansion. Its legacy continues into the twenty-first century as the modern-day Cardinal Newman High School in Forest Acres. In the 1920s and '30s, U.S. Senator Cole Blease from South Carolina would try three times to get Congress to pay the school $112,538 in damages ($60,000 of which went for the cost of the building), citing Sherman's "broken promise." He never succeeded.

An interesting side note is that Sister Baptista's brother was Bishop Patrick Francis Lynch (1817–1882). In 1858, the Irish-born Lynch became the first Catholic bishop of Charleston, South Carolina, to be consecrated in that city. He would serve as bishop for twenty-four years. He was a popular man of the cloth whose sermons impressed a young officer at Fort Moultrie named William T. Sherman.

An avid supporter of the Southern cause, Lynch was named by Jefferson Davis in 1864 as special commissioner of the Confederate States of America to the States of the Church. He went to Europe to attain Vatican recognition of the Confederacy; although he gained an audience with Pope Pius IX, the pope declined the request.

52. Saint Peter's Catholic Church

1529 Assembly Street

The congregation of Saint Peter's Catholic Church was first organized in 1821, in part by the Irish workers who built the Columbia Canal. On the eve of the Civil War, Columbia had a significant Irish community. Though many of Columbia's Irishmen were stoneworkers and manual laborers, there were numerous Irish-born merchants located throughout the city.

St. Peter's Catholic Church Cemetery. Here, Sister Baptista stayed with her charges that cold February night. Appropriately, she was later laid to rest here.

The Irishmen of Columbia would organize themselves as the Columbia Flying Artillery, or Company B of the Third South Carolina Light Artillery Battalion, aka the Palmetto Battalion. The only Irish South Carolina Confederate military unit not based in Charleston, it was attached to the Confederate Army of Tennessee and would see action in Mississippi, Georgia and Tennessee before surrendering at Durham, North Carolina, on April 26, 1865.

The present church was built in 1906 on the site of the 1860s-era church. In its cemetery lay the remains of Major John Niernsee, architect of the current South Carolina State House, and Sister Baptista, who guarded her charges here that cold February night in 1865.

For more information, call (803) 779-0036 or visit www.visitstpeters.org.

53. Richland County Public Library

The main branch is located at 1431 Assembly Street at the southwest corner of Hampton and Assembly Streets

The Richland County Library has been recognized as one of the finest in the nation. Inside the main branch on the third floor is the Walker Local History Room, where researchers can find numerous rare and out-of-print books that deal with the history of Columbia and Richland County.

For more information, call (803) 799-9084 or visit www.richland.lib.sc.us.

Downtown Church Area

Located between Hampton, Lady, Marion and Sumter Streets in downtown Columbia

54. Site of the Gibbes House

Historic marker across the street from the First Baptist Church

Dr. Robert W. Gibbes (1809–1866) was the surgeon general of South Carolina during the Civil War. On January 6, 1865, Gibbes challenged Jefferson Davis's handling of the South Carolina crisis by sending him a telegram that asked him point blank, "Does Jeff Davis hate South Carolina that he means to abandon her to her fate?" Davis replied the next day, "Your dispatch received. My love for your state is equal to the hate our enemy bears it. The subject of your request has my constant care. You know what has been done. If it be possible to do more, the will is not wanting."

During the fire, an old veteran had been posted as a "guard" at Dr. Gibbes's house. By either accident or design, this "guard" quickly fell asleep. Union troops then broke in, looted and burned the dwelling.

Of all the homes and buildings destroyed that fateful night, none was perhaps more tragic from a scholarly and cultural standpoint than Gibbes's. A noted collector and historian, Gibbes lost two hundred paintings, including those by European and American masters, as well as a Renaissance art collection. He lost a large collection of fossils, including a fabulous shark tooth collection, and his collection of documents and papers from the American Revolution and his own impressive private library. The heartbreak from the loss of his collection led to Dr. Gibbes's death the next year.

55. First Baptist Church

1306 Hampton Street

The church was organized in 1809 with Reverend Jonathan Maxcy, first president of South Carolina College, as its pastor. Two years later, it moved into a one-story, forty-foot-square building on the corner of Hampton and Sumter Streets, with the entrance facing Sumter Street. At the time, it was the only brick church in Columbia.

In 1859, a second brick chapel was completed on Hampton Street. Costing $27,000 to build, it could hold one thousand people, about one-seventh of the city's population at the time, and was the largest Baptist church in South Carolina. In this second chapel on December 17, 1860,

First Baptist Church. The Secession Convention first met here on December 17, 1860. Legend states that it was spared the torch due to its sexton's cleverness.

the Secession Convention first met. However, due to a report of a smallpox outbreak at a house across the street, the convention adjourned and reconvened in Charleston.

By far the most famous and popular legend about the destruction in Columbia involves a failed attempt to destroy this church. There are many versions of the story, but the basic tale states that a group of Federal soldiers (in some versions led by Sherman himself) was trying to find the church to burn it to the ground since it had hosted the Secession Convention. Although they were standing right in front of it, they did not find it. They asked a black man, Holland Mitchell, who was passing by, "Where is the Baptist church?" Mitchell, who was the sexton of the church, pointed to a spot and said, "There!"

In some accounts of the story, he pointed to the Washington Street Methodist Church one block down. In other versions, it was the old Baptist sanctuary. Perhaps the Federals were confused as to where he pointed, as both buildings were destroyed, while the chapel that held the convention survived that fateful night.

There are many who dispute the accuracy of this tale, including Sherman. He argued that he was in Columbia for three days and could have found and destroyed the Baptist church easily if he had desired. In an 1865 letter, Mayor Thomas Goodwyn admitted that he had heard the tale but could not verify it. True or not, the second sanctuary continued to serve the members of the First Baptist Church until the 1990s, when it was replaced by a larger facility built next door.

For more information, call (803) 256-4251 or visit www.fbccola.com.

56. Washington Street United Methodist Church

1401 Washington Street on the northeast corner of Washington and Marion Streets

The first church was built on this site between 1803 and 1805. In 1832, it was replaced by the structure that burned during the fire of February 17.

Whether the burning of this church was deliberate or a case of confusion is debatable, but regardless, it was set on fire between 11:00 p.m. and midnight. It took three tries to destroy the building, while the soldiers chanted, "Burn the heathen temple." When Reverend William Conner, the church's pastor, brought a sick child wrapped in a blanket out of the burning parsonage, a soldier grabbed the blanket and threw it into the fire, telling the frightened pastor, "Damn, you, if you say a word, I'll throw the child after it."

The congregation gathered and salvaged as many of the bricks of the burned church as they could and, with clay for mortar, built a small chapel. This temporary structure was used until 1872, when the current Victorian gothic–style building was erected.

Senator Blease tried to get Congress to compensate the church $20,000 to $30,000 for the destruction of its property, citing the legend of Sherman's burning this church because he thought it was the First Baptist. This effort was also unsuccessful.

For more information, call (803) 256-2417 or visit www.gbgm-umc.org/washingtonstumc.

57. FIRST PRESBYTERIAN CHURCH

1324 Marion Street on the northeast corner of Marion and Lady Streets

The first Presbyterian congregation in Columbia was organized in 1795. The members moved the old Lexington County Courthouse building here, on the old public burial grounds. In 1853, the present structure, an early English Gothic design, was built.

The original church's spire, which was seven feet taller than the present one, was the tallest structure in Columbia until 1903. Federal artillerymen used the spire for target practice when they fired their cannons across the Congaree River. Luckily, the church managed to avoid serious damage from the shelling.

The church escaped destruction during the fire, though everything else around it was destroyed. Because of this, many frightened civilians camped in its cemetery during the fire for safety and protection.

The pastor of First Presbyterian, the Reverend Benjamin Morgan Palmer, is the only known clergyman to have fled Columbia. The Charleston native was a popular and persuasive preacher in New Orleans and had been such a key leader in Louisiana's secession movement that friends and family members urged him to leave Columbia for fear that his life would be in danger if he was captured. Reluctantly, he agreed. Though he lost his house and all his belongings in the fire, his family was unharmed.

First Presbyterian Church. The church's spire was the tallest structure in Columbia in 1865 and was used as target practice by Union artillerists. Many Columbians spent the night of the fire in its cemetery.

Buried in its cemetery are the parents of U.S. President Woodrow Wilson; Anne Pamela Cunningham, founder of the Mount Vernon Ladies Association; Ainsley Hall; Jonathan Maxcy, first president of South Carolina College; and two U.S. senators.

In 1920, the church acquired one of the columns intended for the State House that was damaged by Sherman's men. It was erected in the church's cemetery in 1921 and contains the names of eighty-six members of the church congregation who served in the Confederate army.

For more information, call (803) 799-9062 or visit www.firstprescolumbia.org.

The Vista Area

Gervais Street, south of Assembly Street

From the early eighteenth century up to the late twentieth century, this part of Columbia was the heart of its railroad district and an industrial area. In the 1860s, this area was also home to the stonemasons working on the new State House and the local red-light district. According to one Union soldier, the fire that destroyed Columbia began here due to a disagreement between some soldiers and women of ill repute.

58. Wayside Hospital/South Carolina Railroad Depot

800 Gervais on the south side of the street next to Jillian's Restaurant and Wet Willies

The Wayside Hospital was the first of its kind in the world. Started on March 10, 1862, seventy-five thousand wounded soldiers would receive immediate triage care here over the next three years. It was set up along the railroad tracks on Gervais Street at the depot that existed where a restaurant now lies. The train tracks ran on the east side of the building, and the wounded were laid out in the area where the parking lot is now. (An example of this type of hospital can be seen in the depot scene in the movie *Gone With the Wind*.)

On the morning of February 17, the depot held gunpowder, loaded rifles and shells and "every conceivable thing to eat and wear." One of

Wayside Hospital/South Carolina Railroad Depot. The building's explosion on the morning of February 17 literally shook the entire city and killed dozens of people.

the building's guards, C.M. Calhoun, saw inside the building "probably a hundred soldiers and negroes and many white women helping themselves to what they wanted. Most of them had [lit] torches."

As one might imagine, the combination of open fires and explosives proved lethal. It created an explosion so strong and loud that it literally shook the entire city and broke many windows throughout the town. People felt it as far as ten miles outside of the city, and some mistook it for an earthquake. An estimated thirty-five people were killed in the explosion, some literally thrown through the building's roof. After the war, the building was rebuilt from its ruins.

59. Confederate Printing Plant (Publix Grocery Store)

501 Gervais Street, northeast corner of Huger and Gervais Streets

The Charleston printing firm of Evans & Cogswell constructed this building about 1863 to fulfill a Confederate government contract to print money,

Confederate Printing Plant (Publix Grocery Store). Confederate stamps, currency and bonds were printed here, one of the few buildings built to serve the needs of the Confederate government.

bonds and postage stamps. Consequently, it is one of the few surviving buildings built to serve the needs of the Confederate government. Women called "Treasury Girls" did most of the labor for the plant and, in a failed attempt to deter counterfeiting, signed the Confederate currency.

Before Sherman's entry into Columbia, the female workers were evacuated by rail to Richmond, while the plates for printing the stamps and currency were thrown into the Columbia Canal. They have never been recovered. Left behind were millions of dollars in Confederate currency, which, according to Sherman, "our men spent and gambled with in the most lavish manner."

The building was partially destroyed by Sherman's men. After the war, it was rebuilt and purchased by the State of South Carolina for use as a warehouse for the state dispensary from 1895 to 1907. It would remain in use as a warehouse until the 1970s. After lying empty for almost a quarter of a century, the building was renovated in 2004 into a grocery store and condos.

Call (803) 255-4351 for store information.

60. South Carolina Confederate Relic Room and Military Museum and the South Carolina State Museum

301 Gervais Street at the Congaree River

Both of these attractions are housed in the old Columbia Mill, built 1893–1896, the world's first textile plant powered by hydroelectricity.

The Relic Room dates back to the late 1800s, when a room was set aside in the State House to store and display flags and artifacts from the War Between the States. Although the collection has moved several times since then, the name has stuck.

This nationally acclaimed collection contains over four dozen Confederate flags from South Carolina, as well as uniforms, weapons and other items related to South Carolina's role in the conflict. Perhaps the most unusual item is a molar from the mouth of General P.G.T. Beauregard.

South Carolina Confederate Relic Room and Military Museum.

In addition to its War Between the States collection, the museum contains artifacts, mementos and displays from every conflict South Carolina has been in from the American Revolution up to and including the present wars in Asia.

The State Museum, South Carolina's largest museum, tells the cultural, natural and human history of South Carolina from the Ice Age to today. Civil War buffs will especially enjoy the fourth floor, which has a copy of the Ordinance of Secession that was taken by a Federal soldier, who thought he had the original. Also on display is a cannon that was used to defend the city from Sherman, as well as swords, guns and other artifacts from this era.

Admission is required for both attractions. Combination tickets are available.

For tour information for the South Carolina Confederate Relic Room and Military Museum, call (803) 737-8095 or visit www.crr.sc.gov.

For information on the South Carolina State Museum, call (803) 898-4921 or visit www.museum.state.sc.us.

PART THREE

Outlying Areas

Each of the following sites is no more than an hour's drive from downtown Columbia.

City of Columbia

These sites would have been in an undeveloped area outside Columbia's city limits in 1865.

61. Diamond Hill

Monument located in the traffic island at the intersection of Westminister Drive and Stratford Road, off Gervais Street, Columbia

This was the site of the prewar home of Lieutenant General Wade Hampton III. The Greek Revival house had a two-room library consisting of ten thousand books and sat on 108 acres of land. Sadly, there are no known photographs or illustrations of the house. This five-foot-tall marker, erected in 1957, is made from stones that were used in the foundation of the house.

According to several eyewitness accounts, Hampton's home was one of the first things torched by the Yankees on February 17. Since it is several miles from downtown Columbia, there can be no mistake that its destruction was intentional. According to local legend, Major General Phil Sheridan asked Sherman to be sure to burn the Hamptons' houses down. Sheridan had tangled with Hampton at Trevilian Station, Virginia, on June 11, 1864, in an attempt to establish a link between the Federal forces at Charlottesville,

Diamond Hill. The foundation stones are all that remain of Wade Hampton III's prewar plantation home.

Virginia, and General Ulysses Grant's Army outside of Richmond. After two days of fighting, with 1,700 combined casualties, Sheridan retreated in defeat.

According to the tale, "Little Phil" was personally humiliated by this and told Sherman, "When you get to Columbia, be sure to burn that damn Hampton's House." Sheridan looked upon Hampton as a mere "farm boy." A letter from Sherman dated April 8, 1865, from Goldsboro, North Carolina, gives some weight to the legend. In it, Sherman tells Grant to tell Sheridan, "I make him a free gift of all of the blooded [horse] stock of South Carolina including Wade Hampton's whose pedigree and stud are of high repute."

After the war, Hampton moved into his overseer's cabin on the property and built a second home on the site. Called Southern Cross because of its shape, it was a modest single-story framed house with high gables and a small porch. However, Hampton's postwar financial woes forced him to put it up for public auction in 1868 to cover his debts. Because no one had the heart to see the general homeless, he was able to buy back his home and lands for $100.

Bad fortune continued in 1899, when political opponents burned Southern Cross only two weeks before Hampton was to attend a United Confederate Veterans Convention in Charleston. All he could save were his swords, family silver and the clothes on his back. Once again, he moved into his overseer's cottage. Because he was too poor to rebuild, the people of South Carolina took up a collection and built him an even finer home on Senate Street in 1901.

About two miles southeast of this site was the home of Confederate Treasury Secretary George Trenholm, which was destroyed about the same time as Diamond Hill. Nothing remains of the house, and the site is unmarked.

62. French Consulate

2608 Cyprus Street in the Shandon subdivision of Columbia next to the Wheatley Branch of the Richland County Public Library

Little is known about this house, believed to have been built in the 1850s. Originally located at 1924 Main Street, it was a French Consulate office in 1865. French emperor Louis Napoleon III sympathized with the South during the war and granted "belligerent" status to the Confederate States government but stopped short of granting it full diplomatic recognition, a decision that played a role in the upstart nation's demise.

French Consulate. One of only two Main Street structures to survive the fire of February 17, 1865.

According to several accounts, this was one of only two structures left standing on Main Street after the fire. Allegedly, the consulate waved a French flag over this house, saving it from destruction. However, a German principality consulate that was also waving its national colors was destroyed.

About sixty years after the war, the house was moved to 1301 Barnwell Street. In 1977, it was relocated to its present location.

Northeast Richland County

This area was site of numerous health resorts and spas during the antebellum era.

63. Camp Johnston

Historic marker located on Parklane Boulevard between I-20 and SC Highway 277 in front of the Richland County Tennis Center

One mile northwest of this site was a Confederate army training facility, Camp Johnson, at Lightwood Knot Springs near Killians. Once "a summer resort of some note," it served as the Camp of Instruction and later the Bureau of Conscription.

64. South Carolina Department of Archives and History

8301 Parklane Road, in Northeast Richland County, near the intersection of Parklane Boulevard and SC Highway 277

The third largest archive of documents in America and one of the ten most used state archives in America, this collection holds records and documents relating to South Carolina from the colonial era to today. For genealogists and researchers, the archives are a gold mine of information.

For Civil War researchers, there is an extensive number of documents and records for that era. None, however, is more valuable or important than the original Ordinance of Secession, one of the most important and valuable documents in U.S. history. Due to concerns for the document's frail condition, the ordinance is only put on display at certain occasions.

Those interested in the War Between the States who wish to make maximum use of the research facilities may purchase the book *Guide to Civil War Records*, which the archives offers for sale in its gift shop. This book gives a detailed overview of the records the archives holds from the early to mid-1860s.

The Research Room is open to the public. Call (803) 896-6100 or visit scdah.sc.gov for more information.

65. Site of the Skirmish at Killian's

Historic marker located next to the fire station near the intersection of SC Highway 555 (Farrow Road) and Killian Road in northeast Richland County

This marker commemorates a skirmish on February 18, 1865, between Butler's cavalry and elements of the Federal Seventeenth Corps, led by Major General Frank Blair, a congressman-turned-general from Missouri. This action forced Sherman to evacuate Columbia several days sooner than he had planned.

Lower Richland County

Numerous farms and plantations were located in this part of the county during the antebellum era.

66. Kensington Plantation

4001 McCords Ferry Road, near the intersection of U.S. Highway 378 and SC Highway 764, Eastover

Completed in 1854, Kensington is a twenty-nine-room, twelve-thousand-square-foot Italian revival mansion that features a raised basement with a cistern that held ten thousand gallons of water. Originally, the property had 6,600 acres and at least fifty-four outbuildings, though only two of the latter, including the summer kitchen building, survive.

Matthew Richard Singleton, a nephew of a former U.S. ambassador to England, built the house. His father was a major landowner in the area. Singleton's sister, Angelica Singleton Van Buren, was the daughter-in-law of President Martin Van Buren and served as White House hostess during his administration. The house was named after the childhood home of Singleton's wife, Martha Rutledge Kinloch Singleton, near Georgetown,

Kensington Plantation. One of South Carolina's finest and most unique plantation homes.

South Carolina. Wade Hampton III honeymooned here in 1858. The design of the house reflected the family's interest and love of all things European. Despite being born in Charleston, Mrs. Singleton spoke with an English accent and was fluent in French and Italian.

At the plantation's peak, the Singletons owned 465 slaves. One of them, Jacob Stroyer (1848–1909), documented his life at the plantation in his memoir, *My Life in the South*, first published in 1879. A slave cabin still survives, but it is not accessible to the public.

A local legend claims that Sherman had a list of homes to be burned or looted and vandalized in lower Richland County, but Kensington was spared because of its family's matriarch. The story holds that the woman was rocking in her parlor when a soldier came to the front door. She greeted him and begged him to spare her home. Something in the woman's manner impressed the soldier, and he told his men to pass by the house. The legend further states that when Confederate troops came chasing after the Federals, the grateful woman sent the Rebels in the wrong direction to protect her benefactor.

International Paper acquired the site in 1981 and spent two years and $750,000 to restore the house. Since 1996, the house has been furnished with Victorian antiques from the Scarborough-Hamer Foundation.

Kensington Mansion is open to the public. Admission is charged. For more information, call (803) 353-0456 or visit www.kensingtonmansion.org.

67. Millwood

Intersection of Hampton Place and Garner's Ferry Road, across the street from Woodhill Mall, Columbia

Millwood was Columbia's premier mansion in the antebellum era. The original house was built sometime after 1815 by Wade Hampton I as a wedding present for his son, Wade Hampton II, along with fifteen thousand acres of land. In 1838, the younger Hampton started a five-year expansion of his house, turning the four-room house into a one-hundred-foot-long brick mansion. From the porch that surrounded the house, it was said one

Millwood. Six columns are all that remain of what was said to be Columbia's premier plantation home.

could see for twenty-five miles. It was also renowned for its hospitality and the fame of its guests, which included U.S. Senators Henry Clay and Daniel Webster. Contrary to popular belief, it was not owned by Lieutenant General Wade Hampton III but by his sisters, who were affectionately referred to as the "Aunties."

The beautiful mansion was destroyed by Federal troops. Given how far away it is from downtown Columbia, there can be no doubt that the burning of this home was intentional. The family did manage to save its silver and china by wrapping them in curtains and sending them to some family property in York County.

All that remains of the original home are six columns, a wine house and a smokehouse. In the 1960s, the Historic Columbia Foundation stabilized the columns and restored the outbuildings. The Hampton family, who still own five hundred acres, built two postwar frame houses, but they also burned. The current frame house was built in 1922. Descendants of Lieutenant Colonel Frank Hampton, the general's brother killed at the Battle of Brandy Station, Virginia, own Millwood today.

About one and a half miles southwest of this site was another Hampton plantation, Woodlands. The current house, built in 1896, is on or near the site of the original mansion built before 1800 by General Wade Hampton. The original home was also destroyed by Federal troops.

LEXINGTON COUNTY

68. LEMUEL BOOZER HOUSE (KILPATRICK'S/ SLOCUM'S HEADQUARTERS)

320 West Main Street, Lexington

Built circa 1830, this is one of the oldest and most historic houses in Lexington. At the time of the house's construction, the surrounding area was farmland. The home's builder, Lemuel Boozer (1809–1870), served in both houses of the state legislature, as a lieutenant governor and a state circuit judge. Despite being a Unionist, Boozer was mayor of Lexington when Sherman's left wing came through the town. General Kilpatrick chose Boozer's home to be his headquarters on February 15, 1865.

Despite Kilpatrick's promise to Boozer that he would not harm private property and a large number of Unionists living in Lexington, most of the

Lemuel Boozer House (Kilpatrick's/Slocum's headquarters). The presence of two Union generals made this one of the few buildings in Lexington to survive the Union occupation.

town was looted and torched by Kilpatrick's men. The Boozer home was one of the few buildings left standing. The next night, Major General Henry Slocum, commander of the Army of Georgia, used Boozer's home to draw up plans for his army to occupy Columbia.

Slocum (1827–1894) had served at Fort Moultrie, outside of Charleston, before the war and had studied law there with a local attorney. On the eve of the Civil War, he enjoyed a successful legal and political career in New York State. He also led the first Federal troops into Atlanta and Savannah. After the war, he declined an offer to stay in the army, instead returning to New York, where he resumed his career, getting elected to Congress twice.

Slocum's plans for taking Columbia were never used. Though Sherman had planned for weeks for Slocum to take Columbia, he changed his mind at the last moment and had Slocum take his army across the Saluda River, near where the Lake Murray Dam is today, to use Slocum as a feint to protect his true intentions of going to Winnsboro after Columbia.

Professor Joseph LeConte visited Lexington two weeks after the Union troops had left. He found that the town had been erased and "a blacken ruin only remained in its place."

69. Lexington County Museum

231 Fox Street, Lexington

Thirty-six historic structures dating from the 1770s to the Civil War era are on the museum's seven acres. The heart of the museum is the ten-room, two-story John Fox house, built in 1832. Legend states that the daughter of John Fox entertained Union officers in the house by playing the piano. However, her father was strung up three times by Union troops at his nearby plantation in a failed attempt to have him reveal where he buried his valuables.

Lexington County Museum.

Today, the Fox house is furnished to show how a family would have lived in the years leading up the War Between the States. It also features an extensive collection of locally made quilts, pottery and furniture.

For more information about the Lexington County Museum, call (803) 359-8369 or visit www.lex-co.com/museum.

70. Lorick Plantation House (Lake Murray Visitors' Center)

2184 North Lake Drive (SC Highway 6) on the north side of the Lake Murray Dam, just outside the town of Irmo

Built in 1840 by George Lorick, this house was once part of a 7,550-acre cotton plantation. Though the house looked simple on the outside, the interior design reflected Lorick's wealth. Over the years, it was expanded to eleven rooms.

Lorick Plantation House (Lake Murray Visitors' Center).

On the night of February 17, 1865, the Federal Fourteenth Army Corps of the Army of Georgia camped on Lorick's plantation. Officers slept on the second floor, while the first floor was used to butcher and cook cattle. Family legend states that when the soldiers departed they took live coals from the fireplace and spread them over the floor in an attempt to burn the house down. However, fifteen-year-old William Lorick managed to put out the fire. Afterward, young William went to the soldiers' campsite and salvaged some horse corn so his family could eat. This story was repeated many times across South Carolina wherever Sherman went.

The house remained in the Lorick family until 1937. Over the next six years, various owners sold off parcels of the land until Harold Lorick, a descendant of the original owner, acquired the house.

The house was moved twelve miles from its original location to this site in 1995. It was moved in one piece, an action that took seven hours to complete. Today it serves as the Lake Murray Visitors' Center. The exterior has been restored to its antebellum appearance.

For more information on the Lake Murray Visitors' Center, call (803) 781-5940 or visit www.scjewel.com.

Visitors' Information and for Further Research

Those planning to visit Columbia who would like information on area hotels, restaurants and non–Civil War related area attractions should contact the Columbia Metropolitan Convention & Visitors Bureau at 1101 Lincoln Street in the heart of the Vista. You can call them toll free at (800) 264-4884 or locally at (803) 545-0000. You can also visit their website, www.columbiacvb.com.

For Further Research

For more information on Columbia-area Civil War sites listed in the National Register of Historic Places, visit www.nationalregister.sc.gov.

For more information on Columbia-area Civil War sites with historic markers, visit www.scaet.org/markers.

The Historic Columbia Foundation's website has plenty of fascinating information and photographs related to all of Columbia's past. Visit www.historiccolumbia.org.

The Richland County Conservation Commission Cultural Heritage Resources website features numerous sites across the county. Visit www.historicrichlandcountysc.com.

Selected Bibliography

Primary Sources

Anderson, George L., ed. *A Petition Regarding the Conditions in the C.S.M. Prison at Columbia, S.C., Addressed to the Confederate Authorities by Col. John Fraser*. Lawrence: University of Kansas Libraries, 1962.

Armes, William Dallam, ed. *The Autobiography of Joseph Le Conte*. New York: D. Appleton and Company, 1903.

Battles and Leaders of the Civil War. Vol. 4, *Retreat with Honor*. Secaucus, NJ: Castle, 1883.

Brooks, U.R. *Butler and His Cavalry in the War of Secession 1861–1865*. Columbia, SC: State Company, 1909.

———. *Stories of the Confederacy*. Columbia, SC: State Company, 1912.

Bryce, Mrs. Campbell. *The Personal Experiences of Mrs. Campbell Bryce During the Burning of Columbia South Carolina by General W.T. Sherman's Army February 17, 1865*. Philadelphia, PA: Lippincott Press, 1899.

The Burning of Columbia 1. A Letter of Gen. Wade Hampton, June 24 1873 With Appendix II. Report of Committee of Citizens, Ex-Chancellor J.P. Carroll, Chairman, May 1866. From the News and Courier *Charleston, S.C. January 15 & February 5 1888*. N.p.: Walker, Evans & Cogswell Co. Publishers, n.d.

Byers, S.H.M. "The Burning of Columbia." *Lippincotts Magazine*, March 1882.

———. *Iowa in War Times*. Des Moines, IA: W.D. Condit & Co., 1888.

———. *What I Saw in Dixie or Sixteen Months in Rebel Prisons*. Dansville, NY: Robbins & Poore, Printers, Express Printing House, 1869.

———. *With Fire and Sword*. New York: Neale Publishing Company, 1911.

Calhoun, C.M. *Liberty Dethroned*. Greenwood, SC: 1903.

Chesnut, Mary Boykin. *Mary Chesnut's Civil War*. Edited by C. Vann Woodward. New Haven, CT: Yale University Press, 1981.

———. *The Private Mary Chesnut—The Unpublished Civil War Diaries*. Edited by C. Vann Woodward and Elisabeth Muhlenfeld. New York: Oxford University Press, n.d.

Chisholm, A.R. "Beauregard's and Hampton's Orders on Evacuating Columbia—Letter From A.R. Chislon March 23, 1879." *Southern Historical Society Papers* 7, no. 5 (May 1879).

Clark, Thomas D., ed. *South Carolina: The Grand Tour 1780–1865*. Columbia: University of South Carolina Press, 1973.

A Columbia Reader—Edited by the Staffs of the South Caroliniana Library and the Institute for Southern Studies. Columbia, SC: R.L. Bryan Company, 1986.

Conrad, August. *The Destruction of Columbia S.C.—A Translation from the German by Wm. H. Pleasants of the 19th, 20th and 22nd Chapters of "Lights and Shadows in American Life During the War of Secession by August Conrad*. Roanoke, VA: Stone Printing and Manufacturing Company, 1902.

Conyngham, David P. *General Sherman's March Through the South*. New York: Sheldon and Company, 1865.

Copeland, A.C. "Went Through Burning Bridge at Columbia." *Confederate Veteran* 18, no. 4 (April 1910).

Crist, Lynda Lasswell, ed. *The Papers of Jefferson Davis* .Vol. 11. Baton Rouge: Louisiana State University Press, 2003.

Crosland, Charles. *Reminiscences of the Sixties*. Columbia, SC: State Company, 1910.

Dodson, W.C. "Burning of Broad River Bridge." *Confederate Veteran* 17, no. 8 (September 1909).

———, ed. *Campaigns of Wheeler and His Cavalry 1862–1865*. Wheeler's Confederate Cavalry Association. Atlanta, GA: Hudgins Publishing Co., 1899.

———. "More About the Defense of Columbia." *Confederate Veteran* 18, no. 2 (February 1910).

Douglas, David G., with Robert L. Brown. *A Boot Full of Memories*. Camden, SC: Gray Fox Books, 2003.

Ellis, T.H. "Columbia—As Seen by a Rebel Scouting Party the Day After Sherman's Evacuation." *Southern Bivouac* 1, no. 2 (October 1882).

Elmore, A.R. "Testimony About the Burning of Columbia." *Confederate Veteran* 20, no. 3 (March 1912).

Fletcher, William Andrew. *Rebel Private Front and Rear*. Beaumont, TX: Press of the Greer Print, 1908.

Garber, Michael C., Jr. "Reminiscences of the Burning of Columbia, South Carolina." *Indiana Magazine of History* 11, no. 4. December 1915.

Gibbes, Col. James G. *Who Burnt Columbia?* Newberry, SC: Elbert H. Aull Company, 1902.

Thomas J. Goodwyn Papers. Manuscript Collection, South Caroliniana Library, University of South Carolina, Columbia, SC.

Harwell, Richard, and Philip N. Racine, ed. *The Fiery Trail—A Union Officer's Account of Sherman's Last Campaigns*. Knoxville: University of Tennessee Press, 1986.

Hazen, W.B. *A Narrative of Military Service*. Boston: Ticknor and Company, 1885.

Hitchcock, Henry. *Marching with Sherman*. New Haven, CT: Yale University Press, 1927.

Howard, Oliver Otis. *Autobiography of Oliver Otis Howard, Major General United States Army*. Vol. II. New York: Bake and Taylor Company, 1908.

Jones, Katherine M., ed. *Heroines of Dixie: Confederate Women Tell Their Story of the War*. Indianapolis, IN: Bobbs-Merrill Company Inc., 1955.

———. *When Sherman Came: Southern Women and the "Great March."* Indianapolis, IN: Bobbs-Merrill Company Inc., 1964.

Lumpkin, Alva M. *Vignettes of Early Columbia and Surroundings*. Columbia, SC: R.L. Bryan Company, 2000.

McArthur, Henry Clay. *The Capture and Destruction of Columbia, South Carolina February 17, 1865—Personal Experiences and Recollections*. Washington, D.C.: 1911.

Miers, Earl Schrenck, ed. *When the World Ended—The Diary of Emma LeConte*. New York: Oxford University Press, 1957.

Milling, Chapman J. "Ileum in Flames." *Confederate Veteran* 26, nos. 4, 5 and 6 (April, May and June 1928).

Nichols, George Ward. "The Burning of Columbia." *Harpers New Monthly Magazine* 33, August 1866.

———. *The Story of the Great March—From the Diary of a Staff Officer*. New York: Harper and Bros. Publishers, 1865.

Nicholson, William A. *The Burning of Columbia*. Columbia, SC: William Sloane Book and Job Printer, 1895.

Our Women in the War—The Lives They Lived; The Deaths They Died. Charleston, SC: News and Courier Book Press, 1885.

Roman, Alfred. *The Military Operations of General Beauregard in the War Between the States 1861–1865*. 2 vols. New York: Harper & Brothers, 1884.

Russell, D.H. "Last Issue of Confederate Money." *Confederate Veteran* 22, no. 3 (March 1914).

Sanders, Robert W. "Efforts to Capture Charleston, S.C. and Evacuation of the City." *Confederate Veteran* 33, no. 4 (April 1925).

———. "A Long Hard March." *Confederate Veteran* 33, no. 7 (July 1925).

———. "Sherman's Trail Through South Carolina." *Confederate Veteran* 35, no. 3 (March 1927).

Saussey, Clement. "Burning of Columbia." *Confederate Veteran* 17, no. 6 (June 1909).

———. "Two Bridges Burned Near Columbia." *Confederate Veteran* 17, no. 11 (November 1909).

———. "With Wheaton's Battery in the War." *Confederate Veteran* 14, no. 5 (May 1906).

Scott, Edwin J. *Random Recollections of a Long Life: 1806–1876*. Columbia, SC: Charles A. Calvo, Jr. Printer, 1884.

Sea, Andrew M. "Destruction of the Broad River Bridge." *Confederate Veteran* 21, no. 12 (November 1913).

Selby, Julian A. *Memorabilia and Anecdotal Reminiscences of Columbia S.C. and Incidents Connected Therewith*. Columbia, SC: R.L. Bryan Company, 1905.

Sherman, William T. *Memoirs of General William T. Sherman*. 2 vols. New York: Da Capo Press, 1984.

Simms, William Gilmore. *A City Laid Waste*. Columbia: University of South Carolina Press, 2005.

Simpson, Brooks D., and Jean V. Berlin, eds. *Sherman's Civil War*. Chapel Hill: University of North Carolina Press, 1999.

Snowden, Yates. "Marching with Sherman—A Review." Columbia, SC: The State, 1929.

South Carolina Women of the Confederacy. Vol. 1 and 2, *Records Collected by the Committee from South Carolina State Division United Daughters of the Confederacy*. Edited and Published by State Committee UDC. Columbia, SC: The State Co., 1907.

Trezevant, Dr. D.H. *The Burning of Columbia S.C.—A Review of Northern Assertions and Southern Facts*. N.p.: South Carolinian Power Press, 1866.

Upson, Theodore F. *With Sherman to the Sea*. Edited by Oscar Osborn Winther. Bloomington: Indiana University Press, 1958.

War of the Rebellion—A Compilation of the Official Records of the Union and Confederate Armies. 128 vols. Washington, D.C.: Government Printing Office, 1880–1901.

Weiner, Marli F., ed. *A Heritage of Woe—The Civil War Diary of Grace Brown Elmore*. Athens: University of Georgia Press, 1997.

Weller, A. "Sherman Talks Strategy." *Civil War Times Illustrated* 33, no. 3 (July/August 1994).

Wells, Edward. *Hampton and His Cavalry in '64*. Richmond, VA: B.F. Johnson Publishing Co., 1899.

———. *A Sketch of the Charleston Light Dragoons*. Charleston, SC: Lucas, Richardson & Co., 1888.

Whilden, Mrs. Mary S. *Recollections of the War 1861–1865, Mrs. Mary S. Whilden, Charleston S.C., April 1887*. Columbia, SC: The State Co., Printers, 1911.

Who Burnt Columbia?: Official Depositions of Wm. Tecumseh Sherman and Gen. O.O. Howard, U.S.A. Charleston, SC: Walker, Evans & Cogswell, Printer, 1873.

Williams, J.F. *Old and New Columbia*. Columbia, SC: Epworth Orphanage Press, 1929.

Wright, Henry. "'The Awfulest Time I Ever Seen': A Letter from Sherman's Army." Edited by Howard Norman Monnett. *Civil War History* 8, no. 3 (September 1962).

SECONDARY SOURCES

Able, Gene, ed. *Irmo and the Dutch Fork Legacy—A Centennial Celebration*. Irmo, SC: Independent News, 1990.

Baker, Gary R. *Cadets in Gray*. Columbia, SC: Palmetto Book Works, 1989.

Barrett, John G. *Sherman's March Through the Carolinas*. Chapel Hill: University of North Carolina Press, 1956.

Brimelow, Judith M., ed. *South Carolina Highway Historical Marker Guide*. Columbia: South Carolina Department of Archives and History, 1992.

Bryan, John M. *Creating the South Carolina State House*. Columbia: University of South Carolina Press, 1999.

Burning of Columbia Centennial Edition. February 16–17, 1965. Columbia, SC: The State Record Company, n.d.

Calhoun, David B. *The Glory of the Lord Risen Upon It: First Presbyterian Church Columbia South Carolina*. Columbia, SC: R.L. Bryan Company, 1994.

Cisco, Walter Brian. *Henry Timrod, A Biography*. Madison, NJ: Farleigh Dickinson University Press, 2004.

———. *Wade Hampton—Confederate Warrior, Conservative Statesman*. Dulles, VA: Brassey's, Inc., 2004.

Collins, Lisa M. "Historic Gems Tucked Into Lower Richland." *The State*, September 26, 1999.

The Columbia Directory, Containing the Names, Business and Residence of the Inhabitants. Columbia, SC: 1860.

Culberson, David, and Wanda Sightler. "Federals Occupy Lexington." *Lexington County Chronicle* 1, no. 20, February 17, 1993.

Davis, Burke. *Sherman's March.* New York: Vintage Books, 1988.

Destruction of Property in Columbia S.C. by Sherman's Army—Remarks by Sen. Cole L. Blease to U.S. Senate May 15, 1930. Congressional Record 71, No. 8.

Dietz, August. *The Confederate States Post-Office Department.* Richmond, VA: Dietz Press, Inc., 1943.

Edwards, Ann D., George D. Terry, Walter B. Edgar, George C. Rogers Jr. and Augustus T. Graydon. *The Governor's Mansion of the Palmetto State.* Columbia, SC: State Printing Company, 1978.

Elmore, Tom. "The Burning of Columbia." *Blue & Gary Magazine*, Winter 2004.

———. "Camp Sorghum." *Columbia Metropolitan Magazine*, September/October 2005.

———. *"A Carnival of Destruction"—Sherman's March Through South Carolina and the Burning of Columbia 1865.* Charleston, SC: Joggling Board Press, 2011.

———. "Lurid Legends of a Wayward Woman." *Civil War Magazine*, August 1997.

———. "Sherman at Our Door." *Lake Murray Magazine*, August & September 2003.

Fant, Christie Zimmerman. *The State House of South Carolina—An Illustrated Guide.* Columbia, SC: R.L. Bryan Company, 1970.

Faust, Patricia L., ed. *Historical Times Illustrated Encyclopedia of the Civil War.* New York: Harper Perennial, 1986.

Feldman, Michael. *Citizen Sherman.* New York: Random House, 1995.

Franklin, Paul M., and Nancy Mikula. *South Carolina's Plantations & Historic Homes.* St. Paul, MN: Voyageur Press, 2006.

Gandee, Lee R. "Confederacy's Camp Sorghum Was Sordid, Wretched Place." *Columbia Record*, February 15, 1962.

Glatthaar, Joseph T. *The March to the Sea and Beyond—Sherman's Troops in the Savannah and Carolinas Campaign.* Baton Rouge: Louisiana State University Press, 1995.

Graydon, Nell S. *Tales of Columbia.* Columbia, SC: R.L. Bryan Company, 1964.

Hampton, Harry R.E. "Remembrances of Columbia." *Sandlapper—The Magazine of South Carolina* 12, no. 4, April 1979.

Helsley, Alexia Jones. *Lost Columbia: Bygone Images from South Carolina's Capital.* Charleston, SC: The History Press, 2008.

Hennig, Helen Kohn, ed. *Columbia—Capital City of South Carolina.* Columbia, SC: R.L. Bryan Company, 1936.

Historic Columbia's Guide to Historic Columbia. Charleston, SC: Historic Columbia Foundation, 1977.

Hollis, Daniel Walker. *University of South Carolina.* Vol. 1, *South Carolina College.* Columbia: University of South Carolina Press, 1951.

Inkrot, Mary Martha. "A City's Idyll Redefined: Changing Perceptions of the Roles of Parks in the Urban Environment—Sidney Park, Columbia, South Carolina." Master's thesis, University of South Carolina, 1993.

Johnston, Clint. *Touring the Carolina's Civil War Sites.* Winston-Salem, NC: John F. Blair, Publisher, 1996.

Jones, James Pickett. *"Black Jack"—John A. Logan and Southern Illinois in the Civil War Era.* Carbondale: Southern Illinois University Press, 1995.

Lewis, Lloyd. *Sherman—Fighting Prophet.* New York: Harcourt, Brace & World, 1932.

Lord, Francis A. "Camp Sorghum." *Sandlapper* 8, no. 7, August 1975.

Lucas, Marion Brunson. *Sherman and the Burning of Columbia.* College Station: Texas A&M University Press, 1976.

Martin, Samuel J. *"Kill-Cavalry"—Sherman's Merchant of Terror.* Cranbury, NJ: Associated University Press, 1996.

Meynard, Virginia G., *The Venturers—The Hampton, Harrison, and Earle Families of Virginia, South Carolina, and Texas.* Easley, SC: Southern Historical Press, 1981.

Moore, John Hammond. *Columbia & Richland County—A South Carolina Community, 1740–1990.* 1993. Columbia: University of South Carolina Press, 1993.

Royster, Charles. *The Destructive War.* New York: Alfred A. Knopf, 1991.

Seigler, Robert S. *A Guide to Confederate Monuments in South Carolina.* Columbia: South Carolina Department of Archives and History, 1997.

South Carolina—The Works Project Administration Guide to the Palmetto State. New York: Oxford University Press, 1941.

Trinity Church—Columbia S.C., One Hundred and Twenty-Fifth Anniversary. Columbia, SC: The State Company, 1937.

Warner, Ezra J. *Generals in Blue.* Baton Rouge: Louisiana State University Press, 1964.

———. *Generals in Gray.* 1959. Baton Rouge: Louisiana State University Press, 1959.

Wellman, Manly Wade. *Giant in Gray—A Biography of Wade Hampton of South Carolina.* New York: Charles Scribner's Sons, 1949.

Index

About the Author

Photograph by Krys Wood-Elmore.

Tom Elmore grew up in Columbia hearing tales and legends about General William T. Sherman's visit to the city. He has devoted over a decade to researching Columbia's role in the Civil War and has shared his knowledge in bus tours, magazine articles and lectures.

Tom holds a BA in history and political science from the University of South Carolina. He is a book reviewer for *Blue & Gray Magazine* and is on the Board of Directors of the Greater Columbia Civil War Alliance. He lives in Columbia with his wife, Krys, and their two Chihuahuas, Speedy and Sassy.